# CUNARD WHITE STAR
# LINERS OF THE 1930s

The *Majestic* alongside in Southampton
prior to her departure for Rosyth. Note the
cut-down funnels and mast. *HMS Sultan
Museum*

# CUNARD WHITE STAR LINERS
## OF THE 1930s

RICHARD P DE KERBRECH
DAVID L WILLIAMS

CONWAY
MARITIME PRESS

Dedicated to our Mothers, Patricia Teresa and Phyllis Margaret

© Richard P de Kerbrech and David L Williams
1988

First published in Great Britain by
Conway Maritime Press Ltd
24 Bride Lane
Fleet Street
London EC4Y 8DR

ISBN 0 85177 473 3

Designed by Tony Garrett
Typeset by Witwell Ltd, Southport
Printed and bound in Great Britain by
Butler & Tanner Ltd, Frome, Somerset

# CONTENTS

# PREFACE

BACK IN APRIL 1960 a modest little booklet by the late H M Le Fleming entitled *Cunard White Star Liners of the 1930s* was published by Ian Allan at the price of 12½p (2/6d). Large ships of that period have always evoked a nostalgia among shiplovers; perhaps it is the fascination of their sheer size and majesty or the unashamed luxury that abounded during those Depression years. It may even be the fact that the 1930s was the last decade before transatlantic flight became a reality.

At the beginning of that decade the two largest and most prestigious British shipping companies, the White Star Line and the Cunard Steamship Co, were rivals, along with many other foreign shipping companies, on the North Atlantic. Later, against the backdrop of the Great Depression, both companies were to merge in order to survive, forming the Phoenix-like Cunard White Star Line Limited. Subsequent history has shown that in effect the White Star Line was taken over and eventually, in the 1960s, lost its identity completely. The only vestigial remains was its house-flag, flown by Cunard liners up to 1970. Cunard itself is now part of the Trafalgar House Group.

In 1980, to mark its thirtieth anniversary, the Southampton branch of the World Ship Society published an interesting booklet under the title *The White Star Line at Southampton*. Sadly, its limited print run of a mere 300 ensured that every one was a collector's item, denied to a wider and 'hungrier' audience. The authors have long felt that there is a demand for a more detailed book on this subject due to the popularity of these earlier publications. With this in mind we have produced this much more expanded version of H M Le Fleming's 1960 classic.

Our theme is clearly not an unexplored one and much on this subject has been written in the past, but our book is primarily directed at a new generation of liner enthusiasts as well as all who are fascinated by this era. Nevertheless, we hope too that for older shiplovers, already familiar with the events of that time, it will provide a new experience – something of a trip down memory lane, a replay of a favourite old record.

The liners, with the exception of the *Queen Mary*, are all gone now as though they never existed. We hope that through our book we have helped their memory linger a little longer.
**Richard P de Kerbrech**
**David L Williams**

## ACKNOWLEDGMENTS

We would like to extend our gratitude and acknowledgment to the following people and institutions for their kindness in contributing information and illustrations, and without whose assistance this book would certainly not have been written. Wherever possible we have tried to use photographs which are contemporary to the theme of the book and we extend our thanks to the following who contributed the bulk of the photographs: Tom Rayner, a friend of long-standing, whose collection includes those photos taken by the late John McRoberts of Wallasey; John Clarkson; A Duncan; Nigel Overton of Southampton City Museums; John Bell; the Captain of HMS *Sultan* and Lt Cdr Irving Draycott of HMS *Sultan* Museum; Chris Konings of the Netherlands; and the Museum of London. We would also like to thank Peter Thorne for the use of the line illustrations.

We are indebted to Lieutenants K P Hunter and R J Rogers, RN, for their permission to adapt certain passages from their book *HMS Caledonia – The Royal Naval Engineering School – A Short History*. Others who contributed were Southampton Maritime historian Bert Moody, photographic consultant Gerry Packham and Tom Hall.

A typical scene at Southampton's Eastern Docks in the early 1930s. In the Ocean Dock are the *Majestic*, *Berengaria* and *Olympic* with the *Homeric* in the Floating Dock. In the background is Canadian Pacific's *Empress of Britain. Southampton City Museums*

# INTRODUCTION

WHY WHITE STAR and Cunard passenger liners of the 1930s? Simply because this was a crucial decade in the history of these two great British shipping companies. It was a decade which saw them struggling for survival at the outset and which later, in the depths of the economic recession, witnessed their amalgamation under the most difficult circumstances. The company which resulted from this merger was not only better equipped to tackle the problems of that period but turned out to be even more prestigious than either of its parent concerns.

This book is primarily concerned with the ships that made up the respective fleets during that ten-year period and they are described fully in the chapters that follow. First, though, it is fitting to review the contemporary political, social and economic circumstances which together

**The *Berengaria*, initially owned by the Cunard and White Star Companies and named after the wife of Richard I. She was previously the *Imperator*. Tom Rayner Collection**

conspired to necessitate the momentous changes that were forced upon White Star and Cunard.

In the four years following 1929 Britain was in the grip of the Great Depression and world seaborne trade declined by nearly a third. At that time there were more passenger ships afloat to carry fewer travellers than there had been in 1914. Consequently, passenger traffic was equally affected. Every North Atlantic line suffered a sharp drop in passenger receipts, in particular the two major British competitors, Cunard and White Star. The following figures reflect this trend:

| Company | Passengers carried | |
|---|---|---|
| | 1928 | 1929 |
| Cunard | 231,000 | 202,161 |
| White Star | 172,000* | 157,930* |

*Services to Australia not included.

Ocean liners were meeting their schedules but sailing with greatly reduced occupancy. Shipowners were thus faced with the necessity either of severely retrenching or

of going out of business. Most opted for the former and in those lean times hundreds of ships were laid up and many thousands of seafarers laid off.

There were particular reasons why both Cunard and White Star fared worse during the Depression than many of their Continental rivals. The seeds of their difficulties were sown in the years following the end of the Great War.

The political mood of that time, the buoyancy of the victorious combatants, was largely expressed at the expense of vanquished Germany, through a policy of determined economic reprisal, particularly on the part of the French. Following the Armistice, therefore, numerous confiscated German ships became available, ships which were acquired by these British companies in preference to new constructions. The infinitely greater cost of new vessels coupled with protracted delivery times from the then busy shipyards made this option extremely attractive.

When the financial bubble of the Roaring

The *Majestic,* or 'Magic Stick' as she became known, was the largest vessel to be allocated to Britain as a war reparation. She was originally Hamburg America's *Bismarck.* *Tom Rayner Collection*

Twenties finally burst with the Wall Street Crash of October 1929, the weaknesses of this ship replacement policy became apparent. Not only were the Cunard and White Star companies suddenly confronted with drastically reduced demand for their oversize fleets but their front line, express units were ageing and well past their prime. As a result of acquiring second-hand tonnage, neither company had built a major new passenger liner since before World War I. No less than three of the Big Six were ex-German: Cunard's *Berengaria* and White Star's *Majestic* and *Homeric.* All were of pre-war vintage while the other three ships of the group ranged from 15 to 22 years in age.

A further complication was the fact that Cunard and White Star were now also facing stiff competition from a new generation of modern passenger liners introduced by the leading Continental passenger companies. These so-called 'Ships of State' were heavily subsidised and to a large extent shielded from the fullness of the recession's cold draught.

The reparations policy which had been intended to restore the Allies at the expense of Germany seems, in this respect, to have achieved quite the opposite result. Certainly it induced both British companies to adopt what can only be described, with all the benefit of hindsight, as a rather dubious approach to the revitalisation of their fleets.

By the late 1920s efforts were being made to restore the situation and both lines were pursuing ambitious new ship projects. Cunard had been investigating the feasibility of a two-ship weekly express

North German Lloyd's *Columbus* became White Star's *Homeric,* but her reciprocating machinery handicapped her performance as an express liner. She is seen here in Cowes Roads in the Solent. *Tom Rayner Collection*

service for some time and were by then finalising the designs for the first of two monster liners that were described as being 'the smallest and slowest that could do the job'. Meanwhile, the White Star Line had progressed a stage nearer to their goal of realising a new flagship for the transatlantic service. On 18 June 1928

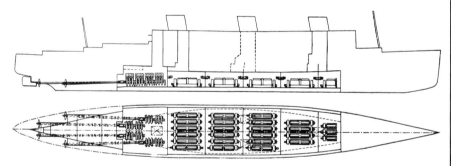

they placed an order with Harland & Wolff, Belfast, for the construction of a mammoth liner which, on completion, would replace the *Homeric.* Laid down as yard number 844 and intended to bear the name *Oceanic,* she would have been the first liner to exceed 1000ft in length. She was the culmination of two years' design work under the leadership of the late Cuthbert Coulson Pounder. The time scheduled for her construction was about 3½ years with the final cost in the region of £3.5 million.

The *Oceanic* was to have measured 60,000 gross tons with an overall length of 1010ft, a beam of 120ft and a draught of 38ft. The quadruple screw vessel would have had 47 six-cylinder, exhaust turbo-charged, four-stroke, single-acting diesel engines capable of producing a total of 275,000ihp which

would have been coupled in pairs to electric generators. This arrangement was designed to give her a speed of 30 knots. The total weight of the installation would have been some 17,000 tons, equal to the displacement tonnage of a smaller liner of the day. The first keel plate was laid down on 28 June 1928 in the Musgrave Yard on Queen's Island.

For White Star, serious financial problems began to develop as early as the spring of 1929 and it soon became apparent that the *Oceanic* had been conceived against an economically fragile background. Initially, work slowed down on the ship which by then had only progressed as far as the completed keel structure. Later, on 29 July 1929, work stopped altogether. The reason given for the stoppage was primarily the rapidly worsening world financial crisis but

it owed more to the fact that the White Star Line could not finance the project on its own. The government was not prepared to forward a loan on such a liner of innovative propulsion plant, especially when it might also be expected to provide a similar loan to the rival Cunard Line, which was about to embark on the construction of its own giant new liner. Consequently, the *Oceanic* project was abandoned and the keel structure discreetly broken up and removed.

Despite this setback for White Star, a month later, on 6 August 1929, the cabin-class liner *Britannic* was launched by Harland & Wolff.

Two days prior to the stoppage on the *Oceanic*'s construction, North German Lloyd's *Bremen* completed her maiden voyage, winning the Blue Riband that Cunard's *Mauretania* had held for no less than 22 years.

White Star may have lost the honours for the first 1000ft liner but, by way of compensation, on 29 November 1929, the keel of a sister ship to the *Britannic*, later to become the *Georgic*, was laid down at the yard of Harland & Wolff at Belfast.

Even as the *Oceanic* project was faltering, Major Frank Bustard, OBE, then White Star's Passenger Traffic Manager, was delivering a lecture to Liverpool's City School of Commerce in which he identified six classes of accommodation provided on the North Atlantic. Changing passenger trends during the 1920s and some of the passenger classifications that were developed as solutions to these problems had a considerable bearing on the prosperity or otherwise of shipping lines at this time. In this context, Major Bustard's observations on social stratification make

interesting reading and are quoted as follows:

(a) First Class by the express steamers from Southampton, used particularly by businessmen and others to whom time is of monetary consideration; also by members of the theatrical profession and film industry who, for publicity purposes, cannot afford to travel other than in the 'monster' steamers.

(b) Some of the companies are still running similar steamers, though not quite so large or fast and at slightly lower rates, from other ports, especially Liverpool. Their patrons are mainly business

**The *Mauretania*. An early view of her moored at the Cunard Buoy in the River Mersey. *Tom Rayner Collection***

travellers and the American tourist class to whom time is not of primary importance and who have learnt by experience the estimable sea-going qualities that prevail on the type of steamer of 20,000–30,000 tons making the passage to or from New York in just over the week.

(c) Cabin Class. This class is supported by many passengers who formerly travelled First Class but who desire to combine economy with their travels, and there are also many travellers who previously crossed Second Class in the three-class ships who prefer Cabin accommodation because there is no better class above them on the ship. The Cabin fares are only slightly higher than the Second Class rates.

(d) Second Class retains its popularity, particularly on the 'monster' steamers.

The *Britannic* of 1930, with her sister the *Georgic*, was the first British motor passenger liner on the North Atlantic run. A rare photo of her on trials on 25 May 1930. *Harland & Wolff*

LEFT: The *Celtic* of 1901 was the first ship to exceed 20,000 gross tons. Together with her three sister ships they became known as the 'Big Four'. *A Duncan*

(e) Tourist Third Cabin is an entirely new class and it is to this particular traffic that the steamship lines look to take the place of the reduced emigration movement brought about by the US Quota Restrictions (United States Immigration Act, 1924). The Tourist Third Cabin quarters afford most comfortable accommodation to passengers to whom economy in travel is the primary consideration, and the development of this travel since 1925 shows clearly the possibilities of an increase in this movement of Americans desiring to visit Europe. Efforts are also being made to encourage the Tourist Third Cabin movement from Great Britain and Ireland to the United States, but it is expected that the bulk of this traffic will emanate from America.

(f) Third Class continues to be maintained more particularly for the emigrant type of passenger and the worker in the United States or Canada when returning home on seasonal or occasional visits.

Although Frank Bustard was a White Star official, his lecture gave a general picture of the classes of accommodation offered by most of the major companies of the day.

During 1929, M J Meehan, a New York stockbroker, ran a trial stock exchange aboard Cunard's *Berengaria*, staffed by two dealers and a wireless operator. Arrangements for communications were made with radio stations at Cape Cod and New Jersey. It was in October 1929, while the *Berengaria* was on passage for New York that news of the collapse of the Wall Street market was received on board. Many passengers were affected financially and it marked the death knell of the floating exchange.

So the 1920s closed on a desperately low note for the world as a whole. The future looked bleak indeed for White Star and Cunard but few at that time could have imagined how the events of the next few years were so drastically to change the destinies of these passenger shipping giants.

# CHAPTER 1
# BEGINNING OF THE ERA —
# CUNARD'S INTERMEDIATE LINERS

AT THE START OF THE 1930s the two largest British shipping companies vied for supremacy on the North Atlantic not only with the major companies of other European countries but also between themselves. Both the White Star Line and the Cunard Steamship Company had large liner fleets offering an almost limitless number of berths, a wasteful abundance that was ludicrous when viewed against the impending era of the Great Depression.

As of January 1930 the White Star fleet comprised the following passenger liners:

| | |
|---|---|
| *Adriatic* | *Doric* |
| *Albertic* | *Homeric* |
| *Arabic* | *Ionic* |
| *Baltic* | *Laurentic* |
| *Calgaric* | *Majestic* |
| *Cedric* | *Megantic* |
| *Ceramic* | *Olympic* |
| *Corinthic* | |

Simultaneously, the Cunard Steamship Company had the following liners on its books:

| | |
|---|---|
| *Alaunia* | *Carinthia* |
| *Albania* | *Carmania* |
| *Andania* | *Caronia* |
| *Antonia* | *Franconia* |
| *Ascania* | *Laconia* |
| *Aquitania* | *Lancastria* |
| *Aurania* | *Mauretania* |
| *Ausonia* | *Samaria* |
| *Berengaria* | *Scythia* |

White Star's fleet included three survivors of the Big Four, namely the *Adriatic*, *Baltic* and *Cedric*, all completed by Harland & Wolff between 1901 and 1906. For some inexplicable reason the *Baltic*, the third of the former quartet, had proved the most popular with passengers. Just over a year before the beginning of the 1930s, on 10 December 1928, the 20,904 gross ton *Celtic* had gone aground off Cobh while in fog and became a constructive total loss. Fortunately, there were no casualties but her demise spelt the end of the Big Four. The three remaining sisters were now entering their last years.

Built around the same time, in 1905,

were the Cunarders *Carmania* and *Caronia* or the 'Pretty Sisters' as they were known. The *Caronia* was propelled by quadruple expansion reciprocating engines while the *Carmania* was the first turbine-driven Cunarder, very much an experiment following the successful demonstration of Sir Charles Parsons' *Turbinia*. Both these liners survived the First World War.

Following World War I it was felt that the era of the big liner was on the wane, and for Cunard especially the post-war reconstruction policy concentrated on the building of a large number of small and medium-sized ships. The first intermediate vessels built for Cunard were the sistership *Scythia*, built in 1920 by Vickers of Barrow, *Samaria*, built in 1921 by Cammell Laird of Birkenhead, and *Laconia*, built in 1922 by Swan Hunter & Wigham Richardson of Newcastle. The *Laconia* was the first British liner to be fitted with

**The *Adriatic*, of the 'Celtic' class. Four masts and two funnels were typical of White Star's early Edwardian era. *John Clarkson, Hutton***

Frahm anti-rolling tanks. All three of the class were propelled by two sets of double-reduction geared turbines which developed 12,500shp, the first in the company to be supplied by super-heated steam. Driving twin screws, this arrangement gave these ships a speed of 16 knots. These Cabin Class Cunarders had a straight stem and no forecastle. Instead they had a small deckhouse between the bow and the bridge front, which supported four lifeboats. The bridge itself was of the island type and had a lifeboat situated on each side while on the main superstructure there were a further twenty lifeboats. The Promenade Deck and 'A' Deck had glass weather screens which enclosed stretches of the decks. At the aft end of the main superstructure, 'A' Deck continued almost to the stern upon which were two more deckhouses each supporting four lifeboats. On 'C' Deck aft there was an opening that extended for some way along each side.

The trio had a total accommodation for 1800 Cabin, Tourist and Third Class passengers, sailing on the Liverpool to Boston and New York service and also on cruises. The Cabin Class were provided with comfortable cabins, many of which had a private bath, a fairly commonplace facility today but a real luxury in the 1930s. The décor of the *Samaria* and *Scythia* was similar but the *Laconia* had a distinctive style of her own. In the two former liners the Writing Room was foremost on the Promenade Deck, and aft of this on both sides of the ship were Garden Lounges enclosed by glass screens, trellis walls, hanging baskets and numerous potted plants. Further aft of the Garden Lounges was a large Oval Lounge topped by a white-painted glass dome in which the colour scheme of the furnishings was gold, grey and vermilion. Situated on the same deck was the Smoking Room which was panelled and fitted with an American Bar.

The Gymnasium was in one of the deckhouses aft, level with the Promenade Deck. The Dining Saloon, which had a capacity for sixty-one tables, was sited on 'D' Deck. The Cabin Class in all three ships had the luxury of lifts from 'D' Deck up to the Promenade Deck and there were also lifts in Tourist Class.

With regard to the *Laconia*, all the public rooms were similarly situated and the Writing Room was also decorated in Adam style. However, the main Lounge, which was square in shape, was furnished in Queen Anne style. The *Laconia*'s Smoking Room was panelled and fitted with a large inglenook which ran for a third of the width of the room. The fireplace was of

**The first liner of the post-war building programme, the *Scythia*. Although built at Barrow, she was completed in Rotterdam owing to industrial trouble at the time.** *John Clarkson, Hutton*

The Samaria, second of the post-war programme, was completed in 1921. She gave a good return on her investment – a service of thirty-five years. Here is a 1955 view of her in Southampton Water. *Tom Rayner Collection*

Bottom: The *Laconia*, built by Swan Hunter, was torpedoed as a troopship in 1942. *Tom Rayner Collection*

The *Carinthia* in cruising colours, white hull with green boot-topping. She is seen in the Mersey during August 1935. *Tom Rayner Collection*

red brick and the whole room was fitted out to give the illusion of an Old English Inn.

Two later sisters to the aforementioned trio and the largest of the class were the *Franconia*, built by John Brown of Clydebank in 1923, and the *Carinthia*, completed in 1925 by Vickers of Barrow. They were also engaged on the Liverpool to Boston and New York run with calls en route at Belfast and Greenock or Cobh and Galway. They were occasionally employed on a service between New York and the West Indies and during the early months of each year they made world cruises of five months' duration, which covered distances of over 35,000 miles with an itinerary that took in some thirty ports. Their external appearance was the same as that of the first three of the class with the exception that the bridge and main superstructure were integral. The extra deck space made available by this arrangement was occupied by two motor lifeboats.

When employed on the North Atlantic mail service the *Franconia* and *Carinthia* sported the normal Cunard livery but for the cruising season their boot-topping was painted green and their hulls white. Both

The *Antonia*, the first of Cunard's 'A' class, in the River Mersey, May 1936. *John Clarkson, Hutton*

vessels were propelled by two sets of Brown-Curtis double reduction geared turbines which developed 12,500shp at 90 rev/min giving them a service speed of 16½ knots.

In both ships the majority of the Cabin Class cabins had a private bath and special attention was given to the matter of ventilation when they were employed on voyages to the tropics. Most of the public

rooms were situated on the Promenade Deck. The aftermost was the Smoking Room which extended two decks high and was decorated in the style of the fifteenth-century Toledo residence of the great Spanish painter El Greco, its walls being adorned by reproductions of his greatest works. Adjacent to the Smoking Room was an American Bar and forward of it was the Lounge, which extended through two decks and was topped by a large central dome, the decor being in Early English style.

Continuing on and flanking the engine room casing were the Garden Lounges, stocked with a surfeit of fine flowers and palms and enclosed by glass windows. Just forward of the Garden Lounges was the Entrance Hall which included the Library and the Chocolate Shop. From the Entrance Hall a lift ran down to 'D' Deck. Forward of the Entrance Hall a corridor divided the Writing Room and the Card Room.

On 'D' Deck was the Dining Saloon, known as the Adam Restaurant, while the swimming pool, gymnasium and squash (racquets) court made up the Sports Arena facility on 'F' Deck, quite an innovation for its day.

More or less contemporary with the *Scythia* class was a new 'A' class trio, comprising the *Antonia*, built by Vickers of Barrow in 1922; the *Andania*, completed by Hawthorn Leslie of Newcastle the same year; and the *Ausonia* built by Armstrong Whitworth of Newcastle. The wisdom of Cunard's decision to build these three vessels was clearly demonstrated by their great popularity with transatlantic travellers. They ran on Cunard's London to Halifax, Quebec and Montreal service in the summer season and on the London to Halifax and St John route in the winter.

**An early photograph of the *Franconia* taken in the River Mersey. *John Clarkson, Hutton***

They were also employed on the Liverpool, Greenock and Belfast to Canada route as well as on the Company's London and Southampton to New York service. They had a well-deserved reputation for outstandingly smart and clean accommodation.

These medium-sized ships had straight stems and counter sterns. They also lacked a forecastle but had a small deckhouse situated rather nearer to the bridge than the stem, upon which were four lifeboats. The foremast was stepped in this same deckhouse. The bridge was of the island type and immediately abaft it was a cargo hatch served by two derricks. The *Antonia* class had a single tall funnel and sixteen lifeboats on the Sun Deck. Below, the

Promenade Deck was open for part of its length but also had glass weather screens. The Promenade Deck continued aft beyond the Sun Deck above, at which point it became open to the weather. In this area were situated the mainmast and four lifeboats.

Below the boats on 'A' Deck was a small opening which continued some way along the ship's side. Further aft, there was a deckhouse which carried another four lifeboats.

The 'A' class provided accommodation for 400 Cabin and 1000 Third Class passengers with, in addition, a large cargo capacity occupying four chambers. The Cabin Class cabins were a notable feature of these

ships; several were fitted with private baths. Among the suite of public rooms was a Smoking Room in Colonial Adam style which had a curved skylight and walnut panelled walls, with an adjoining Bar. The Lounge was large and had a lavender colour scheme with matching furniture. Decorated in French style, the room featured a huge domed ceiling. The Writing and Drawing Rooms were also furnished in Adam style. The Dining Saloon on 'C' Deck extended the full width of the ship.

Steam to the two sets of double-reduction geared steam turbines was supplied by four Scotch cylindrical, oil-burning fire-tube boilers, an arrangement which gave them a speed of 15 knots.

The 'A' class was later added to by a second trio of ships. These were the

*Aurania*, completed in 1924 by Swan Hunter & Wigham Richardson Ltd, Wallsend-on-Tyne, the *Alaunia*, built by John Brown & Co, Clydebank, and the *Ascania*, built by Armstrong Whitworth of Newcastle. The latter pair entered service in 1925.

These three ships were also engaged on Cunard's Canadian services; Liverpool, Greenock and Belfast to Quebec and Montreal during the summer season, with the Canadian terminus switched to Halifax, Nova Scotia, in the winter. In the high season they were also occasionally employed on the London and Southampton to New York service. Their external appearance was virtually identical to the earlier 'A' class trio, the main difference being in the bridge structure. Whereas the earlier ships had a separate island bridge, in the later group it was integral with the

**The *Andania* departing Liverpool.** *Tom Rayner Collection*

The *Ausonia*. *Tom Rayner Collection*

RIGHT: The *Aurania* of 1924, the fourth ship of the 'A' Class, was the first of the post-war Cunarders to have a continuous superstructure. *John Clarkson, Hutton*

The *Alaunia*, built in 1925. *Tom Rayner
Collection*

RIGHT: Bow view of the *Alaunia*. *John
Clarkson, Hutton*

main superstructure. The extra space that
resulted was used for an additional public
room and a large Children's Room.

The *Aurania*, *Alaunia* and *Ascania* could
each accommodate 1000 passengers in
Cabin and Third Class with a crew of 275.
All the Cabin accommodation was of a
high standard of comfort and it included
two suites which comprised twin bedrooms, a sitting room and a bathroom. All
cabins were situated on 'A' Deck. Aft, on

the Promenade Deck, was the Smoking Room which was decorated in Renaissance style and which extended into the deck above. A feature of this public room was a large tapestry on the wall.

Forward of the Smoking Room, on the port side, there was a Bar and a shop, beyond which was the Long Gallery decorated in Old English style, panelled in oak and fitted with indirect lighting which enhanced the room's mellow character. At the after end of the Long Gallery a door led into the Drawing Room which was distinguished by a large dome surrounded by fluted pillars. Adjacent to this was the Writing Room.

At this point there was a division made by the engine room casing, forward of which

**The *Ascania* berthed alongside in Liverpool. The post-war design features are clearly displayed in this view.** *John Clarkson, Hutton*

was the Children's Room with, beyond it still, a large Foyer which in turn led to the Winter Gardens, another domed room surrounded by large windows.

Down below on 'C' Deck the Dining Saloon could seat 281 passengers at fifty-five tables. As with the earlier 'A' class liners, the *Aurania*, *Alaunia* and *Ascania* were also fitted with a large, well-equipped Gymnasium.

Meanwhile, another Cunard liner, the *Lancastria*, had been completed by William Beardmore & Co of Glasgow as the *Tyrrhenia*. She is distinguished as the first Cunarder to be built with a cruiser stern in contrast to the still widespread counter stern that was passing out of vogue during those days. She also had a slightly raked stem. Renamed *Lancastria* in 1924, she was engaged on Cunard's Liverpool to Boston and London to New York services. Later she was also employed cruising. She was the only ship of her class, though a half-

sister to Anchor Line's *Cameronia*.

On her Promenade Deck, forward of the bridge, there were four lifeboats along with the foremast. Working aft from the start of the Promenade Deck was the bridge front, which was of the island type, while abaft the bridge the Promenade Deck was enclosed for much of its length. Above on the Sun Deck there were 24 lifeboats and 2 barges. These latter were sited abreast of the first two, nested, pairs of lifeboats. The mainmast was aft on the Sun Deck.

Down below, the Promenade Deck continued aft for a short distance before it ran either side of two swimming pools. Then it descended to the stern and the docking bridge. 'B' Deck was open right around the stern and as far forward as the end of the Sun Deck.

The majority of the *Lancastria*'s Cabin Class cabins with private baths were on 'A' Deck. Of the public rooms, the Garden

The *Albania*. The cargo-only precursor of Cunard's post-war programme. *Tom Rayner Collection*

BELOW: The *Lancastria* (ex-*Tyrrhenia*) shows her innovative cruiser stern as she departs Liverpool for New York. *Tom Rayner Collection*

The 1905 *Caronia* was like her consort *Carmania*, one of the 'Pretty Sisters'. *Tom Rayner Collection*

Lounge, which was further aft on the Promenade Deck, had a central dance floor on one side of which was a semi-circular bar. Forward of this lounge was a large Gymnasium. The Smoking Room was wood-panelled with a central dome surrounded by pillars. To the port side of the funnel casing and forward of the Smoking Room was the small Writing Room, while on the opposite side of the ship was the Cocktail Bar. These rooms were divided by vestibules leading off from a large panelled Foyer Lounge. From here stairs led down to the lower decks. Down on 'C' deck, the Dining Saloon, which had thirty-eight tables of various sizes, was surrounded by marble pillars which supported the deck above and into which the Dining Saloon extended. The musicians' gallery was on one side.

The *Lancastria* had accommodation for 1300 passengers in Cabin and Tourist Class, and a crew of 300. Her power plant consisted of six double-reduction geared turbines which drove twin screws giving her a speed of 16½ knots.

As has been mentioned, the 'A' class and

the *Scythia* class introduced geared turbines and Scotch boilers to the Cunard fleet. In the case of the *Scythia* class, advantage was taken of the higher steam temperature conditions used and the vessels were fitted with smoke-tube super-heaters to give a steam temperature of 410° F. In the event, these caused so much trouble that they were quickly abandoned and the vessels were operated unsuper-heated.

The *Caronia* as a troopship during World War I, seen here at an Indian port. *Tom Rayner Collection*

The *Carmania*, the first turbine-driven Cunarder. *John Clarkson, Hutton*

# BEGINNING OF THE ERA —
# WHITE STAR'S INTERMEDIATE LINERS

OLLOWING WORLD WAR I, in which it had lost the 48,158 gross ton *Britannic*, one of the three *Olympic* class ships, and five other liners, White Star found its fleet seriously depleted. The Big Four, *Celtic*, *Cedric*, *Baltic* and *Adriatic*, had survived but they were not released from government service until 1919. It became apparent that the Company's immediate priority was a major rebuilding exercise. The inflated post-war building costs discouraged White Star from placing orders immediately and the offer of confiscated German ships ceded to Britain under the Treaty of Versailles looked an attractive alternative. The first ship acquired was the 1909-built, North German Lloyd liner *Berlin* of 16,820 gross tons. She was purchased in November 1920 and renamed *Arabic* after a vessel of the same name lost in August 1915. She was refitted at Portsmouth Dockyard and made her maiden White Star voyage from Southampton to New York on 7 September 1921. The other German liners acquired by White Star, which became the *Homeric* and *Majestic*, are dealt with in the next chapter as part of the Big Six group.

Following the War there was a surge of emigration from Europe to Canada and the United States. To meet this demand, White Star, in conjunction with the

The *Baltic* (left) and *Laurentic* (right) together in port. *Tom Rayner Collection*

The 48,158-ton *Britannic* of 1914 was one of White Star's major losses in World War 1. *Imperial War Museum*

BELOW: The *Cedric* of 1903 had given twenty-seven years of service by 1930. *John Clarkson, Hutton*

American and Red Star Lines, started a service in the spring of 1922 from Bremen, Southampton and Cherbourg to Quebec and Montreal. This service was instituted by the 9,302 gross ton, war-built *Vedic*. During the winter months when the St Lawrence seaway was closed, the west-bound terminals were Halifax and New York. After several months the *Vedic* was replaced on the service by the larger ships *Canopic* and *Pittsburgh*.

By November 1923 Hamburg had replaced Bremen as the European terminal and the former German liner *Arabic* was also employed on this route from 1923, with accommodation for 500 Cabin and 1200 Tourist passengers. However, in the mid-1920s, when the German North Atlantic trade was making a recovery, White Star withdrew from this service. In 1924, the United States Immigration restrictions came into force, causing a big drop in the demand for Third Class passages. This, in turn, resulted in extensive alterations to the passenger accommodation on many ships and the introduction of Tourist Class to attract a new type of traveller.

Contrary to expectations, the big ships did

Another view of the *Baltic* manoeuvring in
the River Mersey. *John Clarkson, Hutton*

Below: White Star's *Arabic* of 1921 was
originally North German Lloyd's *Berlin*,
built in 1909. *Tom Rayner Collection*

not lose their glamour and proved more popular than ever. White Star and Cunard between them possessed five of the six surviving giants and, soon after the war, had the coal-fired ships converted to oil-burning. This permitted a much quicker turn-round in port, besides reducing the number of stokers and trimmers required. The virtual monopoly of these big liners

was, however, short-lived.

The *Doric* of 1923 was of 16,484 gross tons and by contrast with contemporary Cunarders she had two funnels and a cruiser stern. She was built by Harland & Wolff for White Star's Canadian service and launched at Belfast on 8 April 1922. Later, on 8 June 1923, she departed Liverpool on

**The *Doric*, was the only turbine steamer owned by White Star, as completed in 1923 with 'Topliss' davits. *A Duncan***

**The *Doric* following her refit of 1930. *John Clarkson, Hutton***

her maiden voyage to Quebec and Mont-real via Belfast with her initial accom-modation layout providing for 583 Cabin and 1688 Third Class passengers. In 1930 the *Doric*'s accommodation was revised and modified to take 320 Cabin, 657 Tourist and 537 Third Class passengers. The *Doric*'s passenger accommodation spanned four decks. At the top end of the market there were two three-room suites on the Bridge Deck, in which the bedrooms were of Louis XVI period, the walls decorated in pearl grey with white mouldings. Third Class passengers were provided with 2-, 3- and 4-berth cabins which incorporated wash cabinets. Apart from meal times and when the orchestra was not playing in Third Class, the Third Class Dining Saloon doubled as a public room in which passengers had the use of a piano and a gramophone for entertainment.

In addition to passengers the *Doric* had a cargo capacity of 439,148 cubic feet in nine holds served by eight hatches.

The *Doric* was, in fact, the first and only turbine-driven liner ever built for White Star. She had two sets of Brown-Curtis turbines, single-reduction geared to twin screws and giving a service speed of 15½ to 16½ knots.

By comparison, the *Laurentic*, which entered service four years later, returned to the triple-screw propulsion arrangement of twin triple-expansion steam recipro-cating engines exhausting to a low pressure turbine. The *Laurentic* was slightly larger in tonnage and beamier than her near sister the *Doric* and was capable of carrying 600 Cabin, 400 Tourist and 500 Third Class passengers. She sailed on her maiden voyage from Liverpool on 12 November 1927.

Other liners on the Canadian service were the 16,063 gross ton *Calgaric* and the 18,940 gross ton *Albertic*. They were, re-spectively, the former *Orca* and *Ohio* of the Royal Mail Steam Packet Company and they were transferred to White Star in February 1927 to augment the *Laurentic* on the Canadian route. However, the *Calgaric*, which started on her first trip from Liver-pool on 4 May, spent long periods laid up and was finally switched to cruising from Southampton early in 1931.

The *Albertic* had originally been laid down as the *München* for North German Lloyd before being ceded to the Royal Mail

**The *Laurentic*, built by Harland & Wolff at Belfast for the Canadian service. She was destined to be the last coal-burning transatlantic liner built.** *Tom Rayner Collection*

The *Megantic. Tom Rayner Collection*

Bottom: The *Albertic* passed to White Star in 1927 and was formerly Royal Mail's *Ohio*. She had originally been laid down in 1914 as the *München*. *John Clarkson, Hutton*

The *Megantic*, assisted by tugs, berthing at Liverpool. *John Clarkson, Hutton*

Steam Packet Co as the *Ohio* in 1923. She was originally placed on the Liverpool to Canada service for White Star, from February 1927. However, when the *Laurentic* entered the service that November she displaced the *Albertic*, which was then sent south with the *Megantic* to inaugurate a new service from London, Le Havre and Southampton to Quebec and Montreal. In this manner both vessels called at Southampton in either direction on this fortnightly service and in this connection the *Megantic* called at Southampton for the first time on 22 March 1928.

In 1929, the *Albertic* returned to Liverpool and was replaced by the *Calgaric*. The service to Canada lasted some four years but the curtailment of emigration caused it to close.

Following the entry into service during

1927 of the *Albertic* and *Calgaric*, plans were drawn up by White Star for a new Cabin Class ship and in 1928 the Big Four, the *Cedric*, *Celtic*, *Baltic* and *Adriatic*, were also converted to Cabin Class.

**The *Calgaric* was originally completed as a cargo vessel in 1918. *Tom Rayner Collection***

The *Adriatic*, last of the Big Four to be built
and a knot faster than her sisters. Her
available IHP had also been increased by
2000. *Tom Rayner Collection*

# CHAPTER 3
# THE BIG SIX — GERMANY'S LOSS, BRITAIN'S GAIN

FROM THE POINT OF VIEW of North Atlantic operations, the Wall Street Crash occurred near the end of the 1929 season and had little impact on balance sheets for that year. In fact, 1929 was the highpoint for passenger carrying since the end of World War 1.*

The 'crunch' for the British lines came during the 1930 season when the figures for all First Class passengers showed an alarming decline. Cabin Class appeared to be not too greatly affected while those for

*See Appendix II

**RIGHT: Albert Ballin's three giants together at Southampton on 27 July 1930; the** *Leviathan, Majestic* **and** *Berengaria.* *Authors' Collection*

**The entry of North German Lloyd's** *Bremen* **gave Cunard and White Star extra competition on the Atlantic route in addition to the impending Depression.** *J Elder*

46

Tourist Class even showed an increase. This last figure looked well enough on paper but was not as encouraging as it first appeared. Although the fashion for Tourist Class was spreading, it was becoming equally apparent that a good deal of the gain was being made at the expense of the higher priced accommodation. In other words, the trend was not so much one of new passengers being attracted as of regular travellers being tempted to cross at a cheaper rate. This trend was far from what the major companies wanted as it was on their First Class clientele that they relied for their main revenue.

Despite this fall off, in May 1930, Cunard announced that John Brown of Clydebank had been appointed to construct a new liner which was to be over 1000ft long and which was to form the basis of a new two-ship express service in place of the existing three-ship service. Cunard and White Star already had between them five of the world's nine largest liners of the day and, prior to the advent of the *Bremen* in 1929, United States Lines' *Leviathan* and French Lines' *Ile de France* were the only non-British registered liners in the top eight. Cunard had the *Aquitania* and *Berengaria*, while White Star owned the *Olympic*,

**The *Mauretania*, the famous record breaker, combined power and elegance. Her speed meant hard work for stokers. *Tom Rayner Collection***

**The *Mauretania*, 'The Old Lady of the Atlantic'. *John Clarkson, Hutton***

*Majestic* and *Homeric*. Known collectively with the *Mauretania* as the Big Six, their background was as colourful as that of their owners.

The 30,704 gross ton *Mauretania*, a sister ship of the *Lusitania* which had been sunk in World War I, was launched in September 1906 at Swan Hunter & Wigham Richardson's yard at Wallsend-on-Tyne. She sailed on her maiden voyage on 16 November 1907 and soon after gained the Atlantic Blue Riband. In appearance, the main distinguishing feature between the two liners was in the type of ventilators on either side of the funnels. Those of the *Mauretania* were of the huge cowl type and as a result her profile was not as uncluttered as that of the *Lusitania*, which had smaller ventilators. Both ships were extremely luxurious in their interior fittings. The *Mauretania* was the faster of the two and, although the Blue Riband record passed between them several times, the *Mauretania* established her superiority in 1909 with a crossing at an average speed of 26.06 knots. She went on to hold the record for the next twenty years and, even though she was twenty-two years old when finally beaten by the *Bremen* in 1929, the *Mauretania* produced better speeds in defence of the title than those with which she had first captured it.

Originally, the *Mauretania* maintained Cunard Line's express service from Liverpool to New York in consort with the *Lusitania*. In October 1914 she was commissioned by the Admiralty for use as an auxiliary cruiser but as she proved to be

unsuitable she was laid up temporarily. However, she did see plenty of active service during World War I, first as a troop-

**The *Olympic*, the only survivor of the pre-World War I trio. Her wartime trooping duties earned her the title of 'Old Reliable'. She is seen in the Solent outward bound for New York c July 1914. *Courtesy Marilyn Averis***

ship, then as a hospital ship and later again as a troopship after the United States' entry into the conflict in 1917. Her trooping service ended in May 1919 and, after a short refit, she resumed commercial sailings in March 1920, based at Southampton instead of Liverpool. Following a fire in 1921, the *Mauretania* was sent back to her builders for a complete overhaul and for conversion to burn oil fuel. This

work was completed in March 1922 and she then returned to the express service, working alongside the *Aquitania* and the newly acquired *Berengaria*. In June 1929 the *Bremen* took the Blue Riband from her but she fought back, making an eastbound passage at 27.22 knots. What is not readily appreciated is that when the *Mauretania* was built it was before the era of single- or double-reduction gearing and the turbine

The *Aquitania*. Between the World Wars it is believed that she carried more passengers than any other transatlantic liner. *Tom Rayner Collection*

rotors were actually directly coupled to the screw shafts. Therefore, the speed of revolution of the turbine rotors was in effect the same as that of the propellers, allowing for minor transmission losses.

From 1930 onwards the *Mauretania* was employed almost exclusively on cruises and, befitting this new role, she was painted white.

The 45,324 gross ton *Olympic* was the first of a trio of great liners ordered by the White Star Line in reply to the Cunard Line's *Mauretania* and *Lusitania*. The *Olympic* was laid down in December 1908 on a slipway at Harland & Wolff's Belfast yard especially constructed for the three

ships. As originally designed the *Olympic* and *Titanic*, the second ship, were to have had three funnels and four masts but, as completed, their fourth funnel, a dummy, gave them an attractive and balanced profile. The *Olympic* was launched on 20 October 1910 and revitalised the name that had been intended for the projected but cancelled sister ship of the *Oceanic* of 1899.

Eight months later, on 14 June 1911, she began her maiden voyage from South-ampton. On 11 September the same year, while outward bound for New York, she collided with and damaged the cruiser HMS *Hawke* in the Solent. The *Olympic* was holed in her starboard side near the stern and, with her voyage cancelled, she returned to Belfast for repairs. Following the *Titanic* disaster in April 1912, the *Olympic* returned once more to Belfast for extensive alterations to improve her water-

tight integrity and to have additional life-boats fitted. This raised her gross tonnage to 46,440.

When World War I broke out, the *Olympic* continued to make commercial sailings and on one such voyage, on 27 October 1914, she gave assistance to the crippled battleship HMS *Audacious* which had struck a mine in the Irish Sea. However, the warship sank before reaching port. Soon after this incident the *Olympic* was laid up at Belfast but she was requis-itioned for trooping during September 1915. She performed this task throughout the rest of the war. On 12 May 1918, while approaching France fully laden with troops, she was attacked by the German submarine U103 whose torpedoes missed her. In pressing home the attack the sub-marine had ventured too close for its own safety and the *Olympic* managed to ram and sink her adversary.

BERENGARIA PASSING CALSHOT.

The *Berengaria* (*c* 1928) outward bound
from Southampton, passing RAF Calshot.
Note 'erks' attending floatplane on slipway.
*John Bell Collection*

The *Olympic* returned to commercial work
in July 1920 following a refit which
included the conversion of her furnaces to
burn oil fuel. In 1922 she was joined on
the New York route by the *Majestic* and
the *Homeric* and the White Star Line was
able to operate a somewhat unbalanced
three-ship express service for the first
time. At the beginning of the 1930s the
*Olympic* was the largest British-built ship
and remained so until the advent of the
*Queen Mary*. She was also the world's
largest triple-screw liner. Her unique com-
bination of quadruple-expansion steam
reciprocating engines exhausting to a low-
pressure turbine also gave her the record
for the largest low-pressure marine turbine
ever constructed.

In 1922, the *Berengaria* entered the
Trafalgar Drydock, Southampton. The
liner's stern overhung the caisson and there
was only ten inches between her hull and the
dock walls. *Authors' Collection*

The 45,647 gross ton *Aquitania* was ordered as a third ship for Cunard's express mail service but her construction, unlike that of the *Lusitania* and *Mauretania*, was not assisted with government money and consequently the ship was built to a more economical design. Her dimensions and passenger accommodation were greater than the earlier pair but her speed was markedly reduced. She was one of the last of the pre-World War I giants. Laid down in June 1911, the *Aquitania* was launched on 23 April 1913 by Lady Derby. Her building costs totalled £2 million.

The *Aquitania* began her maiden voyage from Liverpool on 30 May 1914 and had

**The *Berengaria* (left) outward bound and the *Majestic* inward bound pass St Helens Fort off Bembridge, Isle of Wight, *c* 1924. *Authors' Collection***

**Cunard's *Berengaria* prior to her 1922 refit. She is identified here as 'Cunard's *Imperator*'. To Sotonians she became known simply as the 'Berrie'. *Authors' Collection***

hardly got into the stride of the transatlantic service when World War I interrupted her schedules. She was subsequently taken over for conversion into an Armed Merchant Cruiser but damage sustained in a collision when nearing completion demonstrated that she was too big and unmanoeuvrable for active service and a full conversion was therefore suspended. During 1915 and 1916 she worked first as a troopship and then as a hospital ship in the Gallipoli campaign, after which she spent a short spell laid up. From 1917 onwards she was used to carry United States troops to France. The *Aquitania* was returned to Cunard in 1920 and immediately reconditioned and converted to oil fuel before returning to commercial duties.

She maintained Cunard Line's Southampton to New York express service throughout the 1920s and into the 1930s,

**The first arrival at Southampton of the *Majestic*, 22 March 1922, seen here approaching the Ocean Dock. *Southern Newspapers Ltd***

The White Star steamship *Majestic*, the
biggest vessel in the world, had its smoke
stacks divided so that they passed up the
sides of the vessel instead of the middle. By
this arrangement the spaciousness of the
saloons was enormously increased. *Authors'
Collection*

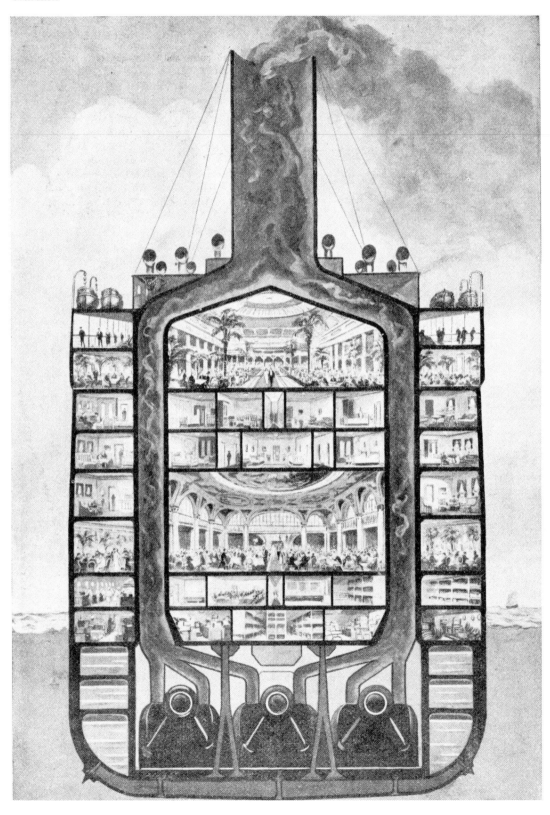

and, apart from occasional cruises, ran in consort with the *Mauretania* and *Berengaria*.

The *Berengaria*, still bearing her original name *Imperator*, joined the Cunard fleet in April 1922 but her pedigree was wholly Teutonic. In the early years of the twentieth century the Hamburg America Line (HAPAG) embarked on a policy of building larger, more luxurious liners of lower speeds rather than out-and-out greyhounds specifically to break records. This culminated with the *Imperator* trio. Built as an answer to the White Star giants, the three HAPAG ships remained the world's largest until the advent of the *Normandie* in 1935. Their interior decorations were superb and from their external appearances they were magnificently massive. They were, however, reported to be structurally weak and difficult to manoeuvre. Although they were the pride of all Germany only two of the trio were destined to sail under that flag and for less than two years at that. In fact, the last of the three ships, the *Bismarck*, never made a voyage for the Hamburg America Line.

Construction of the *Imperator* began in August 1910. The original intentions were for her to be named *Europa* but she was launched in May 1912 in the presence of the Kaiser and fittingly christened *Imperator*. She made her maiden voyage from Cuxhaven to New York fifteen months later. The *Imperator* suffered from a number of teething troubles when she entered service of which the most serious was poor stability. In 1913 she was taken in hand to cure this and other problems and her funnels were shortened by 9ft in an attempt to reduce top weight.

As built, the *Imperator* had a huge figure-head on her bows of a German eagle surmounting a globe. Designed by a Professor Bruno Kruse this was later removed, probably when the other alterations were effected, and replaced by a simple scroll work crest. Barely a year after she had entered service World War I broke out and the *Imperator* was laid up safely in the River Elbe. Her sister, the *Vaterland*, was less fortunate, having been in New York at the commencement of hostilities. The *Imperator*'s luck was relatively shortlived, however, for when Germany signed the

Armistice with the Allies she was handed over to them as a war reparation.

Until August 1919 the United States used her as a troopship between Europe and the United States, ferrying home American troops after which she was laid up at New York until transferred to Great Britain in 1920. The Cunard Line then operated her on the North Atlantic run as a replacement for the *Lusitania* until February 1921 when they bought the *Imperator* and her sister ship the *Bismarck* in a joint deal with the White Star Line. The object of the exercise had been to avoid outbidding each other and the arrangement was that ownership of the two vessels would remain shared for the next ten years. In effect, therefore, the *Berengaria* and *Majestic* were the first Cunard White Star ships, reverting to separate ownership for only three years.

Cunard sent the *Imperator* to the Tyne for

**White Star Dock (renamed Ocean Dock in 1922), Southampton, showing the express service Cunarders *Berengaria*, *Aquitania* and *Mauretania*; also White Star's *Adriatic*. Authors' Collection**

reconditioning and conversion to oil fuel and she emerged as the slightly larger *Berengaria* in April 1922. One very distinctive alteration was the placing of six of the twelve lifeboats, previously carried under each side of the Promenade Deck on 'A' Deck, up onto the Boat Deck abaft the middle funnel. The remaining six were lifted during a refit in the late 1920s.

A drydocking operation in the Trafalgar Drydock at Southampton during 1922 involved the *Berengaria* in a bit of a drama. A large vee notch had been hewn in the drydock wall in order to accommodate part of her bows but when she entered the drydock there was still very little clearance at the sides and ends of the liner. Even though the bows were hard up against the fender, only about eight inches was left between the rudder and the drydock caisson. Along the sides of the vessel the clearance was also very small. With a displacement tonnage of around 63,060 (52,022 gross tons) the *Berengaria* had to be lightened as much as possible to facilitate docking and in order to achieve this her lifeboats were put ashore. The docking was carried out by John I Thornycroft & Co, with the assistance of Cunard Line staff. The task was all the more remarkable when one considers that it was carried out by apprentices and labourers because a strike was in progress in the shipyard at the time.

When the *Majestic* made her maiden voyage from Southampton on 10 May 1922, the White Star Line finally had its three-ship express service. The *Majestic* had originated as the *Bismarck*, the third of the Hamburg America Line's giants, and in a way represented the end of an era herself for she was the last of the mammoth liners planned before World War I. In fact, the war prevented her completion as conceived and so shattered the dream of Albert Ballin, the head of HAPAG, for a three-ship North Atlantic service. The *Bismarck* was laid down in 1913 and launched by the late Chancellor Bismarck's grand daughter, the Countess Hanna von Bismarck, on 20 June 1914. At the climax of the ceremony she experienced some difficulty in breaking the champagne bottle on the *Bismarck*'s hull. To spare her

blushes, the Kaiser, who was also present for the naming ceremony, stepped forward and broke the bottle for her.

The outbreak of war interfered with the *Bismarck*'s completion as all shipyard labour was diverted to more urgent German war effort. So she languished in an incomplete state during the War until, in 1919, the British Reparations Commission awarded her and the *Imperator* to Great Britain to replace the sunken *Britannic* and *Lusitania*. As stated previously, the *Bismarck* was bought under a package deal for joint ownership by the Cunard and White Star Lines but as Cunard were already operating the *Imperator*, the *Bismarck* became the White Star ship. Aided by Harland & Wolff officials, White Star Line then tactfully set about supervising the completion of the *Bismarck* to their own specifications at the Blohm & Voss shipyard at Hamburg. The Germans were understandably reluctant to part with her but 1200 shipyard workers nevertheless completed her construction.

When the White Star crew arrived at Hamburg during March 1922 to take the *Majestic* on her trials in the Irish Sea they found the liner alongside the dock painted in Hamburg America Line livery and displaying the name *Bismarck*. On board, the Master found his cabin being used for the storage of ship's fittings. Furthermore, they found that Royal suites had been built into the *Bismarck* to carry the entire German Imperial family on a round-the-world victory cruise. Members of the German public and the shipyard workers were reputed to have lined the dockside and the banks of the River Elbe in silence when the *Majestic* eventually sailed from the port.

While the ship was at sea, a short re-naming ceremony was performed and she arrived at Southampton in White Star colours and bearing the name *Majestic*. Her name well described her appearance and she looked all of her 56,551 gross tons. She resembled the *Leviathan* (ex *Vaterland*) rather than the *Berengaria* and, like the *Leviathan*, she had the boiler uptakes divided and taken up the sides of the ship to rejoin below the funnels. This configuration gave a vast, uninterrupted, area of open space on the

Promenade Deck and was used to great advantage in her magnificently decorated public rooms. Her interior space was said to be equivalent to 400 eight-roomed houses. She had nine steel decks, the five lowest running the full length of the ship. These lower decks were sub-divided into compartments containing watertight doors controlled from the bridge. The ship's hull consisted of a double bottom of cellular construction and of great strength. Above the fifth deck were the four decks which contained the cabins and public rooms, the lengths of which occupied the middle third of the liner.

The swimming bath, to cite just one luxury amenity, was in the Pompeian style of Ancient Rome. It was furbished with rich marbles and brilliant red mosaics and had an area of 820 square feet and a depth ranging from 3 to 9 feet. The First Class Dining Saloon was also the Central Hall and spanned two decks. It could seat 600 to 700 passengers in one sitting. It was surrounded with tall windows which helped illuminate the lofty frescoed dome which was supported on slim ionic pillars.

The *Majestic* had an overall length of 956ft, a beam of 101ft and a depth from the keel to the Boat Deck of 101ft. She was powered by four German-built Parsons type turbines. Her 240 furnaces were oil burning and fired 48 boilers. The engines developed 100,000shp which gave her a maximum speed of 24 knots and made her the second fastest of the Big Six. She had also been fitted with Frahm anti-rolling tanks, a modification of the Flume stabilisation system.

During August 1922 the *Majestic* anchored in Cowes Roads alongside the Royal Yacht *Victoria & Albert* and was inspected by King George V during his visit to the Cowes Week regatta. The *Majestic* was to remain the world's largest liner for thirteen years.

White Star's *Homeric* made her maiden voyage from Southampton to New York on 15 February 1922 but she proved a slow ship for an express service and was difficult to fit into a regular timetable. The *Homeric* had started her career as North German Lloyd's *Columbus* and as such she was launched on

**The *Homeric* was employed on odd cruises. On a 'Cruise to Nowhere' in 1931, fares started from three pounds. From 1932, she was switched to full-time cruising. *A Duncan***

17 December 1913 at the F Schichau yard at Danzig (now Gdansk). By the time World War I broke out she was virtually complete but her owners considered it to be prudent to leave her in this advanced state of construction, laid up at a safe enough distance from the arena of conflict so that she could be made ready for service as soon as the war ended. Unfortunately, for both Germany and North German Lloyd, the outcome of the war was not as anticipated and the *Columbus* was accordingly awarded as a war prize to Great Britain. The final stages of her construction were carried out in the Danzig shipyard and on her completion, in 1920, she was handed over to the British Shipping Controller.

At this time the White Star Line had been reorganising their fleet for peacetime service and needed new ships to replace those lost in the war, notably the *Olympic*'s second sister ship, the 48,158 gross ton *Britannic*. Since the loss of the *Titanic* in 1912 they had had a 40,000 gross ton ship projected as a replacement. Apparently she was at first to have been known as the *Germanic* but after the outbreak of war the name was prudently changed to *Homeric*. However, in 1921 the

White Star Line decided to abandon this project and buy confiscated German tonnage instead. They thus acquired the *Columbus*, gave her the name of their projected liner and set about modifying her to their own specifications. In 1924, two years after her acquisition, she was converted from coal to oil fired furnaces in the hope that it would improve her speed performance but this made little difference. In 1930, the *Homeric* was the world's largest twin-screw liner and the largest to be propelled by steam reciprocating machinery.

*Note: According to Frank Braynard's* Leviathan – Volume II, *the* Leviathan *was measured at 59,956 gross tons under British gross tonnage measurement regulations, making her the largest liner in the world. By comparison, the* Majestic's *measurement of 56,551 gross tons was based on the original German calculations made before the vessel had been altered to burn oil instead of coal. Had she, perhaps, been remeasured according to the British regulations her gross tonnage would have been nearer to 62,000. Further to this, the late N R P Bonsor states in* North Atlantic Seaway – Volume II, *published in 1978, 'For several years subsequently, the American-owned* Leviathan, *commissioned in 1914 as the 54,282 ton* Hamburg America Vaterland, *was advertised as having a tonnage of 59,956 but a different and unorthodox basis*

*of calculation was used (to arrive at this figure) and there is no doubt that the* Majestic *was the larger ship. When it suited them the American company reduced their tonnage claim to 48,943!'*

*The importance of this must surely be lost to the modern-day reader but it reflects the conflict between the earning power of prestige on the one hand and the extra running costs in pilotage, navigational marks and berthing levies, all based on tonnage, on the other. To some extent the practice of manipulating tonnages continues and for much the same reason, but the recent introduction of standardised measurement should ultimately mean that there will be a realistic relationship between a liner's dimensions and carrying power, and its registered tonnage in all cases.*

# CHAPTER 4
# WHITE STAR MOTORSHIPS —
# THE KYLSANT INFLUENCE

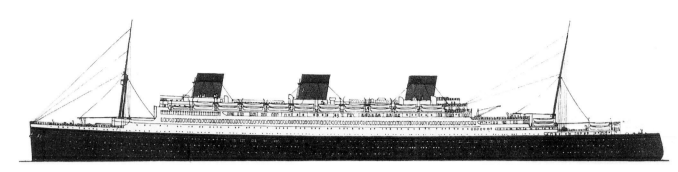

I T IS PERHAPS WORTHY of note that each of the three main phases of White Star's history was characterised by some distinctive feature of the fleet. The first phase, under the Ismay family's control, was marked by early express liners; the second – when the White Star Line came under the control of J P Morgan's International Mercantile Marine – by slower, larger and more luxurious liners; and final period – the Royal Mail

phase – by the building of diesel-powered vessels. Lord Kylsant, the Chairman of the Royal Mail Group, was a champion of the motorship and from the moment he gained control of it he planned the inclusion of motor vessels in the White Star fleet. It was against this background that the *Britannic* and her later sister, the *Georgic*, were conceived but while they reflected an outstanding trend of the 1920s and 1930s in being innovative motorships, they

J H Isherwood's profile of White Star's proposed *Oceanic*. The concept metamorphosed into the smaller liners *Britannic* and *Georgic*. *J H Isherwood*

Royal Mail's *Alcantara* (foreground) was a precursor to the motor vessels built by Harland & Wolff for White Star Line. In the background, the *Berengaria* is in the floating dock which came to Southampton in 1924. *Tom Rayner Collection*

**The *Britannic* in the River Mersey during her maiden voyage. The era of the big motorship had arrived.** *Tom Rayner Collection*

equally represented an important trend in being three-class Cabin ships.

The accommodation they provided set a new standard for Cabin Class ships of the day. The most noteworthy features were the swimming pool, tennis courts, the beautiful two-decks high Louis XIV Dining Room, the provision of lifts for all classes and a Children's Playroom in both Tourist and Third Classes. There was a picturesque Card Room in the French style of the late Gothic at the forward end of the Promenade Deck. The Lounge which was also on the same deck was in the late-eighteenth-century English style which had been given a contemporary flavour by the inclusion of full-length pier glasses and beautifully varied furnishings. Cinema 'Talkie' apparatus, modern for the day, was

installed and a resilient parquet floor was also provided for dancing. Leading from the Lounge to the Smoking Room was a tastefully decorated Long Gallery which formed a pleasant promenade area when the weather was bad. The Drawing Room which was in Old Colonial style with Adam flavour also doubled as a place for religious services, the altar being situated in the same public room. The Smoking Room was a detailed reconstruction of a Tudor room in an Elizabethan mansion coupled with the luxury of modern furniture. Outside the Smoking Room was the Verandah Café.

The *Britannic* measured 26,493 gross tons and was driven by twin H&W–B&W ten cylinder, 4-stroke, double-acting oil engines which developed 20,000 maximum bhp at 110 rev/min and gave a service speed of around $18\frac{1}{2}$ knots. At the time of her inauguration she was the largest and most powerful motorship in Britain. The Chairman of Harland & Wolff claimed that

she could move 'one ton one mile on a thimbleful of oil' – very economical for its day.

In addition to four 500kW diesel generators, the *Britannic* had a standby 75kW diesel generator if for any reason the main sets were out of action. The Engineers' Smoke Room was situated in the forward funnel.

A double bottom extended the full length of the ship in which was stored fresh water, fuel oil and water ballast. The *Britannic* was also sub-divided into thirteen watertight compartments. All auxiliary machinery was electrically driven, there being over 7000 lights installed on the liner. The Galley ovens were also electrically heated.

The *Britannic* had a capacity for 1550 passengers in Cabin, Tourist and Third Classes. She left Liverpool on 30 June 1930 on her maiden voyage to New York via Belfast and Glasgow, during which she

A fine view of the *Britannic*. Developments in 4-stroke diesel propulsion were perhaps stretching the abilities of marine engineers to run and maintain such machinery. *Courtesy Cunard*

averaged 17.04 knots. The appearance of the *Britannic* was also unique, her two squat motorship funnels starkly contrasting with the tall, natural draught funnels of the steamships of the day. As with other new Cabin Class liners being brought into service during the time of the Depression, the *Britannic* proved a popular ship and she maintained a full quota of passengers trip after trip while other ships were crossing half empty. In fact all the new Cabin liners that entered service during that economically inclement period were among the few vessels that continued to carry full loads of passengers It was well known that the newest ships attracted the most customers. The *Bremen*, in 1929, and the *Europa*, which entered service in the same year as the *Britannic*, showed this, but with respect to the Cabin Class ships there was more to it than that. The modern Cabin ships were certainly not as fast as the express liners but they provided practically everything else at lower fares, and in less prosperous times that was a determining factor for the seasoned traveller. The *Britannic*'s cheapest fare was £19 one way. Nevertheless, despite the proven popularity of the *Britannic*, the White Star Line operated at a loss of £379,069 for the year ending December 1930 for the very first time, a very sad state of affairs.

The *Britannic* preparing for her maiden voyage from Liverpool. *John Clarkson, Hutton*

The *Georgic* was the last liner to be built for White Star and her completion heralded the end of that Company's connection with Harland & Wolff. *A Duncan*

The *Majestic* in her heyday passing the Battery, downtown Manhattan, bound eastward for Europe. *Southampton City Museums*

BELOW: The *Majestic* arriving at Southampton. *Courtesy C Konings*

The *Majestic* at the Ocean Dock,
Southampton, prior to departure.
*Southampton City Museums*

**A pre-1927 view of the *Majestic* in the Floating Dock.** *N V Robinson Collection*

**The *Berengaria* in Southampton's Floating Dock, having just completed an overhaul, *c* 1931.** *John Bell Collection*

Another view of the *Majestic* high and dry in the Floating Dock at Southampton. In the New Docks in the background is the *Olympic. Frank Braynard*

Another view of the *Majestic* high and dry in the Floating Dock at Southampton. In the New Docks in the background is the *Olympic. Frank Braynard*

# CHAPTER 5

# 1930-32 — THE LEAN YEARS

O N 11 JANUARY 1930 the 16,786-ton *Arabic* made her first eastbound crossing from New York to Cobh and Liverpool, having reverted to White Star after three years on Red Star Line service. She could carry 177 Cabin, 319 Tourist and 823 Third Class passengers. Later, on 15 March, she made her first voyage from Liverpool to New York.

The same month, Cunard's *Albania*, which had been completed by Scott's Shipbuilding & Engineering Co Ltd of Greenock in 1920, was disposed of. She had been built for maximum cargo capacity with only a limited accommodation for eighty Cabin Class passengers. The staterooms were located on the Shelter and 'Tween Decks. The *Albania's* hybrid design had proved to be

**The *Albania's* hybrid design proved unsatisfactory compared to her consorts. She was sold to Italian interests during 1930. A rare photograph of her underway. *Tom Rayner Collection***

**BELOW: The *Albania*, a cargo-passenger vessel, could carry eighty passengers. She was laid up in 1925. *A Duncan***

unsatisfactory compared to that of the other vessels of the 'A' class and she had been laid up since 1925. In March 1930 she was sold to Navigazione Libera Triestino and renamed *California*.

The *Arabic's* contribution to White Star schedules turned out to be very shortlived. Later during 1930 she was laid up after completing only five round voyages, her last trip having been made on 16 July.

As 1930 drew to its close the keel of Cunard's giant express liner was laid down at John Brown's shipyard on Clydebank as yard number 534, later to become the *Queen Mary*. An air of cautious optimism prevailed but the writing was on the wall, for only a million passengers had crossed the Atlantic that year.

If 1930 witnessed a decline in passenger traffic, then 1931 saw a virtual collapse, for

westbound passenger receipts alone decreased by 240,000 and the unpleasant fact emerged that the British lines were losing more passengers than their Continental rivals. The tendency was for passengers to book aboard the latest ships in service and the German liner *Europa* carried some 500 more passengers per trip than any other liner on the run. Then again, the Continental companies had the benefit of state subsidies which of course the Cunard and White Star Lines did not.

Around this time Cunard instituted short four-day cruises from New York to Bermuda and Halifax. The liners on the express service normally spent five days in New York between voyages so Cunard decided to utilise this time by employing the giant liners on these short cruises. The fares were made as cheap as possible, from £10 upwards. The bonus for travelling

**The *Ceramic*, for years the largest ship sailing between Europe and Australia. *John Clarkson, Hutton***

Americans, in the midst of the Prohibition era at home, was that alcoholic drinks could be obtained aboard the British ships. The cruises proved very popular with the liquor-starved American passengers, so much so that White Star followed suit. So it was that the 'Four Day Whoopee Cruise' or 'Booze Cruise' became quite an institution on the eastern seaboard of the United States as a cheap and fun weekend at sea, at least for those who could afford them. Calls were made at the British-owned ports in order to exploit a legal 'loophole' in compliance with US Navigation Laws which forbade foreign ships from trading directly between United States' ports.

Besides being a major British company on the Atlantic service, White Star Line also had a stake in the Antipodes trade. Their 18,481 gross ton *Ceramic* was at the time the largest ship on the Australian run and remained so until the advent of the *Dominion Monarch* in 1939. She had a very large deadweight tonnage of 19,590 which included a refrigerated capacity of 321,000

cubic feet. In addition to this she had accommodation for 820 Cabin Class passengers. She was propelled by triple-expansion steam reciprocating engines exhausting to a low-pressure turbine and driving triple screws and giving a service speed of 15.5 knots. A centrally placed single funnel and four masts gave her a similar appearance to the Big Four. White Star's route to New Zealand in the 1930s was maintained by the *Ionic* and the *Corinthic* in conjunction with Shaw Savill & Albion's *Mataroa* and *Tamaroa* which operated a four-weekly run from Southampton to New Zealand via Panama taking 32 days. The *Corinthic* was sold on 16 December 1931 for breaking up at Hughes, Bolckow & Co, Blyth, but the following year was scrapped at Wallsend. At the same time the *Ionic* was converted to take 280 Tourist Class passengers only.

During June 1931 Cunard's *Franconia* was chartered by Furness Withy & Co, to take the place of the *Bermuda* which had caught fire while lying at Hamilton, Bermuda and

whose superstructure had been left badly damaged. The *Franconia* was chartered for five months during which time she was utilised on the New York to Bermuda run, pending the entry into service of the *Monarch of Bermuda* on 28 November that year.

In July 1931 Lord Kylsant was tried for fraud at the Old Bailey and was jailed for 12

**The *Ionic*, White Star's vessel on the London-New Zealand service. In 1927 she rescued the crew of the French sailing ship *Daisy*. *Tom Rayner Collection***

months. He had been arrested on charges under the Larceny Act and found guilty on one charge of issuing a false prospectus and not guilty on two counts of issuing false annual reports and accounts.

In the same month the 1909-built *Megantic* was laid up in Rothesay Bay, pending disposal. Earlier that year she had reverted to the Liverpool to Quebec and Montreal route from her previous London based service to Montreal, via Le Havre, Southampton and Quebec.

Also, in July and September 1931, Cunard's

**White Star's *Corinthic* ran in conjunction with Shaw Savill's *Mataroa* and *Tamaroa*. She was scrapped during 1932. *N V Robinson Collection***

*Carmania* and *Caronia* were laid up at Tilbury after 26 years' service, their fate uncertain. That September the *Homeric* was used as an accommodation ship during the Schneider Cup seaplane trophy race which took place over the Solent that month, giving a hint that her future too was open to speculation. Prior to that, during the August bank holiday weekend the *Homeric* sailed

from Southampton on a 'cruise to nowhere'. In fact the cruise took her to Southern Ireland and back, the fares for the mysterious trip ranging from £3 to £7/7/0d.

The *Britannic*'s slightly larger sister was launched on 12 November 1931 with the name *Georgic*. Although similar to the earlier motorship, the one major external difference between them was in the shape of the superstructure beneath the bridge; on the *Georgic* it was rounded while on the *Britannic* it was squared. Although not appreciated at the time the *Georgic* was in fact the last White Star liner ever to be built.

As 1931 drew to a close White Star showed a further financial loss of £450,777; even the sale of the former German liner *Arabic* to

**The *Franconia* was chartered in 1931 for five months by Furness Withy for the New York to Bermuda service. This photo shows her in the River Mersey during June 1936. *Tom Rayner Collection***

Italian shipbreakers at Genoa for £17,500 and of the *Cedric*, the second-built of the Big Four, for £22,150, did little to offset this deficit.

Worse was to come for, on 11 December, work on the new Cunarder 534 building at John Brown's at Clydebank was suspended. She was already in a fairly advanced state of construction and it had been hoped to launch her in May 1932. The Depression was spreading throughout the country and the financial situation for Cunard was getting worse. They had spent £1.5 million to date on building No 534 and the prospect for raising further monies in the market looked bleak. Their gross revenue for 1931 had been around £2.5 million less than for 1930, resulting in a net loss of £533,204.

The Chairman, Sir Percy Bates, edicted that all Cunard staff 'from the directors down' would have to take pay reductions. This and other economies were expected to save Cunard at least £1,780,000 a year. With

regard to North Atlantic passenger and freight traffic, there was still a glut of tonnage and plenty of foreign competition. Confronted with this and with no foreseeable assistance forthcoming, Cunard was left with no alternative but to order the cessation of work on their new liner. Three thousand men directly employed on its building were laid off and a further 10,000 in subcontracted industries throughout the land, such as rolling mills, foundries, and pump manufacturers, were also made jobless as a result. Despite this state of affairs in Britain, across the Channel at the Penhöet yard in Saint Nazaire, work on the new French liner was proceeding to schedule.

From the very start of 1932 events continued on a low note for both companies. On 11 January the *Cedric* sailed from Liverpool for the scrapyard at Inverkeithing, having made her last voyage the previous September and the *Homeric* also made her last Atlantic crossing that month, following which she was switched to full-time

The *Carmania* was the first turbine-driven ship built for Cunard. The success of this installation led to its adoption in the *Lusitania* and *Mauretania. Tom Rayner Collection*

BOTTOM: The *Megantic*, which started 1931 by operating on the Liverpool to Quebec run, was laid up the same July. *Tom Rayner Collection*

cruising: a wise decision as events were to prove for that year.

Because of the prolonged lean spell on the North Atlantic older units such as the *Carmania* and *Caronia* were put on the disposals list by Cunard. The 'Pretty Sisters' had been both completed for Cunard in 1905 and in doing so Cunard made an experiment of building two ships exactly alike except for their method of propulsion. The *Carmania* was the first turbine-driven ship built for the company while the *Caronia* had installed what were regarded as more conventional quadruple-expansion reciprocating engines. In this manner a comparison of the two systems was made. The success of installing steam turbines, in terms of operating efficiency as well as greater increase of speed and economy in the *Carmania*, influenced Cunard's decision to further employ this type of machinery in its later *Mauretania* and *Lusitania*.

These earlier two-funnelled, twin-masted Edwardian liners were noted for their graceful elegance of interior layout. In 1914 the *Carmania* became an Armed Merchant Cruiser, in which capacity she gained notoriety for fighting and sinking the German liner *Cap Trafalgar*.

So in January 1932 the *Caronia* was sold for scrap to Messrs Hughes Bolckow Shipbreaking Co for £20,000 for delivery in July although subsequent events gave a sinister twist to her ultimate fate. The *Carmania* was sold to shipbreakers at Blyth during April.

Early on 11 June, the *Georgic* was completed by Harland & Wolff at Belfast. Born at the height of the Depression, her entry into service was a defiant gesture. She had the distinction of being Britain's largest motor liner with a gross tonnage of 27,759. Although not known at the time, her début brought down the curtain on the long association between Harland & Wolff and the White Star Line, the *Georgic* being the last liner to be built for them. The *Georgic* had accommodation for 479 Cabin, 557 Tourist Class and 596 Third Class passengers. With regard to her interiors the *Georgic* was well equipped for her day and had luxury in her Tourist and Third Classes

which could not have been considered possible even in First Class prior to 1914. Of her First Class amenities she boasted a Pompeian style swimming pool and modern cocktail bar. She had a cruiser stern and a slightly raked stem and the forward end of the Promenade deck was rounded off in the form of an Observation lounge. Like the

The *Georgic* preparing for her maiden voyage from Liverpool, 25 June 1932. *Tom Rayner Collection*

Britannic, the *Georgic*'s forward funnel was a dummy and contained the Engineers' Smoking Room as well as the wireless cabin. The *Georgic* commenced her maiden voyage on 25 June sailing from Liverpool for New York. On the outward voyage she made an average speed of 16.46 knots while homeward bound she averaged 17.72 knots.

In September, the *Homeric* was involved in a minor collision with the Spanish-registered cargo ship *Isla de Teneriffe*. Neither ship was seriously damaged and they were both able to proceed on their respective voyages.

A month later, on 3 October, the *Laurentic* was involved in another minor collision

**The *Georgic* departing on her maiden voyage on 25 June 1932. She was built mainly to cater for the Cabin Class passenger.** *Tom Rayner Collection*

while on a voyage between Quebec and Liverpool. The collision, with the Belfast steamship *Lurigethan*, occurred in fog sixteen miles east of Point Amour at the western entrance to Belle Isle Strait. The damage to both vessels was, however, only superficial and above their water lines, and they were able to continue about their business.

A strange event occurred a month later in November 1932 when the *Caronia*, which

had been sold previously to Hughes Bolckow for shipbreaking, was resold to Japanese shipbreakers for £25,000 plus £14,000 for delivery to Japan. She sailed for Japan under the name *Taiseiyo Maru*.

This in itself seemed harmless enough, for Japan, without its own iron ore for steel production, had always relied on the scrap metal market for this resource. At the time, however, Japan was at war with China and, although its purpose in buying old ships was

**The *Cedric* became a victim of rationalisation, having given almost thirty years of service to her owners.** *Tom Rayner Collection*

The *Laurentic. A Duncan*

BOTTOM: The *Baltic*, photographed in the
River Mersey during April 1929, followed
the parade to the breakers in January 1933.
*Tom Rayner Collection*

primarily to recycle the scrap steel, there were rumours that the *Caronia* might be used as a troop transport in that conflict. In the event she was not.

The Japanese, in fact, purchased many other redundant liners and in January 1933 the *Baltic*, the third of the Big Four, was also sold to them for breaking up, sailing from Liverpool for Osaka on 17 February 1933

under her own steam. The *Megantic*, which had been laid up at Rothesay Bay for eighteen months, also sailed to Osaka for scrapping the same month. There was no doubt but that these liners could have been used as transports had the Japanese so wished, although there was a stipulation in the sales contract in each case that the ships were to be broken up and used for nothing

**Cracks appeared in the *Olympic*'s port crankshaft at the end of 1932 which caused her to be withdrawn from service for three and a half months. *A Duncan***

**The *Carinthia*'s World Cruise in January 1933 covered some 40,000 miles and included more than forty ports. *A Duncan***

else. It is most probable anyway that the scrap metal was of greater value to Japan at that time than the ageing ships, which had seen better years, would have been for military purposes.

Returning to 1932, the Cunarder *Carinthia*, which had been refitted in London for a world cruise, left Southampton on 14 December for a short cruise to the West Indies. Later, on 7 January 1933, she left New York on her world cruise on which she steamed some 40,000 miles and visited more than forty ports. The itinerary included the remote island of Tristan da Cunha.

Yet another liner to make news cruising in December 1932 was the *Homeric*. Earlier that month she became the first liner to berth at Southampton's (still incomplete) New Docks Extension. On 21 December she made the first departure from the New Docks when she too sailed on a Christmas cruise.

In fact, 1932 was a boom year for cruising with more than 100,000 Britons spending their holidays at sea. During that period more than 200 cruises were operated from British ports. It was not surprising, therefore, that Cunard and White Star joined in the competition and even the *Olympic* sailed on Bank Holiday cruisers from Southampton with fares as low as £3 per head.

Towards the end of the year the *Olympic* developed a small fracture in her port engine during a homeward-bound voyage. Following this her subsequent sailings were cancelled and her machinery surveyed. The rumours spread that the *Olympic* was about to be withdrawn from service and scrapped. Instead she was given a three month overhaul. In the course of this her accommodation was updated to take 618 First, 447 Second and 382 Third Class passengers. (It had previously been 675 First, 561 Tourist and 819 Third). While the *Olympic* was out of service, the *Georgic* was switched from Liverpool to operate from Southampton in her place. The *Olympic* resumed her services on 1 March 1933.

White Star's losses for the year 1932 amounted to £152,045 – a depressing end to a depressing year.

**Southampton's Eastern Docks *c* 1933. Cunard's *Aquitania* is on berth 47, *Mauretania* is on 43 and *Berengaria* at 44. On berth 46 is White Star's *Majestic*, with *Homeric* outside. In the Trafalgar Drydock is Canadian Pacific's *Empress of Australia* while on 32-33 berth on the Itchen Quays is the *Empress of Britain*. Blue Star Line's *Arandora Star* is in the Empress Dock and on berth 34 is Royal Mail's *Alcantara*. Courtesy Malcolm Wayman**

# CHAPTER 6
# 1933 — OPTIMISTIC DAWN

B Y COMPARISON, THE start of 1933 was somewhat better. Negotiations were entered into between the National Government and the Cunard and White Star Lines with respect to the sleeping mammoth on the stocks at Clydebank. In October of the previous year, Neville Chamberlain, then Chancellor of the Exchequer, had asked Lord Weir to conduct a confidential enquiry into the trading and financial positions of British shipping companies operating mail and passenger services on the North Atlantic and to make a special survey of building and operating subsidies paid by foreign governments to their national operators. He took just eight weeks to deliver his secret report and 27 years later he said of it: 'It was my firm belief that the British Government should guarantee a building loan to the Cunard company on condition that the two companies [Cunard and White Star] merged into one, united front against the

**The *Albertic*. A Duncan**

opposition.' This report was to pave the way to an amalgamation of the two rivals and the forwarding of a government loan to complete No 534.

Even as the Weir report was being submitted the political wind of change was blowing throughout Europe with Adolf Hitler appointed Chancellor of Germany on 30 January 1933.

During March the 18,940 ton *Albertic*, the former Royal Mail Line's *Ohio* of six years earlier, was laid up in the Holy Loch pending disposal. Three months later, in June, the motorship *Britannic* made a record voyage at an average speed of 19.5 knots with the largest number of passengers carried by any Atlantic liner that year, a total of 1,103.

At Southampton, the large 1,200ft graving dock which had been built to accommodate the new Cunard liner was opened by King George V and Queen Mary on 26 July 1933. The Royal Yacht *Victoria & Albert* sailed into the flooded basin to perform the

opening ceremony. Later, the Southern Railway Company and civic dignitaries took a special train from the new drydock to the *Berengaria*, berthed in the Ocean Dock, where they had lunch. Meanwhile, the King and Queen sailed aboard the *Victoria & Albert* for Cowes and the opening of regatta week.

Among other less sensational happenings during the year, the *Laconia* carried a record consignment of 41,000 cases of grapefruit, apples and plums from New York and Boston to Liverpool. During the same month, the *Mauretania* left Havana bound for New York returning from a cruise and made the 603-mile voyage at an average speed of 27.78 knots with 112 miles steamed at an average of 32 knots:

Between 12 and 29 August the smaller, 16,063 ton White Star vessel *Calgaric* was chartered to undertake a cruise for the Boy Scouts and Girl Guides Association. The party consisted of 100 Scouts, 475 Guides and 80 non-Scouts or Guides.

The *Berengaria* hosted the Civic Luncheon after the opening of the King George V Graving Dock in July 1933. Southampton taxi drivers dubbed her 'The Dead'n Bury Her'. *John Clarkson, Hutton*

The *Calgaric* was recalled from Canada especially to make the cruise. When she sailed from Southampton on 12 August, on board were the Chief Scout and Chief Guide, Lord and Lady Baden-Powell. The cruise took them to the Baltic states of Latvia and Estonia before returning via Oslo and the north of Scotland to terminate at Liverpool. It proved to be a highly successful cruise, so much so in fact that the last of the Big Four, the *Adriatic*, was chartered by the Boy Scouts Association for the same purpose the following year. However, on 31 August 1933 the *Adriatic* was laid up at Liverpool. Ironically, at about the same time the wreck of her sister *Celtic*, which had gone aground at the entrance to Cobh Harbour and which posed a threat to shipping, was finally cut up by oxy-acetylene torches where she lay.

The following month, on 3 September, the *Calgaric* was laid up at Milford Haven, while later, on 30 September, the Cunarder *Carinthia* received an SOS from the Latvian steamer *Andromeda* which had struck a submerged object 80 miles west of Ushant and which later sank. Although the *Carinthia* diverted her course in order to render assistance, she resumed her course on hearing that the steamer *Hartside* had already saved the crew of the stricken ship.

ABOVE: The *Laconia* carried more grapefruit than passengers in 1933. *John Clarkson, Hutton*

Two months later, on 15 November, the *Berengaria* was also in receipt of an SOS, this time from the British steamer *Saxilby* which was sinking in the Atlantic with a crew of 27 on board. The *Berengaria* altered course but upon reaching the reported position of the sinking ship she found no trace of the *Saxilby* nor any survivors or lifeboats.

As 1933 drew to its close, there were definite signs that the worst of the slump was over. There was an improvement in the price of steel and consequently of scrap metal and many British shipowners took the opportunity to dispose of their surplus tonnage at the elevated scrap value. The general improvements in the financial conditions in Britain had been brought about by trade agreements concluded during the year. However, there was no great improvement in the North Atlantic trade where the competition of the newer, palatial Cabin ships had cut into the profits of the more expensive express liners and these had, for the most part, run at a considerable loss. White Star's losses for 1933 amounted to £353,552.

At the end of the year, in December, one of the new Cabin liners in question, the *Britannic*, ran aground in Boston Harbour in dense fog, although without damage. She had only 250 passengers on board at the time and was refloated after twelve hours.

From express liner to full time cruise ship. The *Mauretania* is seen here in white cruising livery. *A Duncan*

When built in 1901, the *Celtic* was the largest ship in the world. Sadly, she did not survive into the 1930s. *John Clarkson, Hutton*

'Bon Voyage'; the *Calgaric* departing Southampton on 12 August 1933 on her Baltic cruise for the Scouts and Guides Association. *B A Butt*

In September 1933 the *Carinthia* answered an
SOS from a Latvian steamer, the *Andromeda*.
*Tom Rayner Collection*

AS AN INDICATION that the worst of the Depression was over, on 9 January 1934 the *Franconia*, which the previous year had been re-decorated throughout at great expense, left New York for a five-month world cruise covering some 37,500 miles. The fares started from 305 guineas (£315/5/0d). By sailing day 400 passengers who were prepared to pay the price had booked aboard her. Meanwhile, around the same time, the *Samaria* was scheduled to operate on a series of ten cruises from Tilbury. On 19 January, the *Majestic* became the first ship to use the new King George V Graving Dock at Southampton. During her early days with White Star she had been drydocked by the United States Navy at their drydock at the Boston Navy Yard. Later, from 1925, she was able to use the Southern Railway's 60,000-ton floating dock which was moored off Southampton's Town Quay. It had not been possible for her to enter the Trafalgar dry dock at Southampton because she was some 37ft longer than the *Berengaria* which herself experienced a very close fit when she entered it in 1922, as mentioned earlier.

Another Cunarder which also underwent a three-month refit during 1933 was the *Aquitania*. In the course of it a 'talkie' cinema system was installed and the ship was generally rejuvenated after 19 years in service. The job provided work for 1000 men. The new year had not begun well for the *Aquitania* for on 26 January she had gone aground on Calshot Spit at the entrance of Southampton Water. She was refloated after 2½ hours with the assistance of tugs from Southampton.

Two months later, the *Adriatic* was chartered to take a large party of Boy Scouts on a Mediterranean cruise between 19 March and 15 April. Another special cruise was undertaken by the *Laurentic* in March when she left Dublin for Italy with seven hundred pilgrims on board. They were due to arrive in Rome on Easter Monday to witness the ceremony of closing the Holy

**On 19 January 1934, the *Majestic* became the first liner to use the King George V Graving Dock at Southampton. *Hulton Picture Library***

During 1934, the *Franconia*'s five month
World Cruise indicated that the Depression
was on the wane. *A Duncan*

Door in Saint Peter's Church by Pope Pius
XI. For the voyage ten altars were fitted in
the *Laurentic* to cater for the many priests
on board. A cinema was also fitted for
entertainment during the trip.

Under the North Atlantic Shipping Act of
1934, which was passed in the House of
Commons on 27 March, the British
government proposed to lend a sum of £9.5
million to a merged company of the Cunard
and White Star Lines. This comprised £3
million for the completion of No 534, £1.5
million working capital and £5 million
towards the construction of a sister express
liner. To this end the Cunard White Star
Line Limited was formed on 1 January 1934
to take over the trade of the two former rival
companies, now partners for all future
services. Cunard was allocated 62 per cent of
the capital and White Star 38 per cent. The
merger effectively brought an end to the
White Star Line. The new company was
registered on 11 May with a working capital
of £10 million in £1 shares. One week after
the Bill was passed in the House, the sound
of rivetting guns and caulking hammers

**The *Franconia*, seen here in 1954, was
completed in 1923. Her upperworks were
continuous, without an island bridge
structure. *Tom Rayner Collection***

The *Majestic* in the King George V Graving
Dock. *John Bell Collection*

could be heard reverberating in the large hull on Clydeside – work on 534 had resumed in earnest.

A sad note during this transition period from rivals to partners occurred on 16 May, when, in thick fog, the *Olympic* rammed and sank the Nantucket Lightship moored in the approaches to New York harbour. The seven-man crew of the lightship were all drowned in the accident and subsequently the US government claimed $0.5 million compensation.

There was better news in June when the *Aquitania* made a record passage of 5 days 13 hours and 40 minutes at an average speed of 23.92 knots, quite an achievement for her after twenty years of service.

In July the official transfer of the registry of the ships took place, White Star's contribution to the new company being ten ships. These were the *Majestic, Olympic, Homeric, Georgic, Britannic, Adriatic, Albertic, Laurentic, Doric* and *Calgaric*. Upon the merger, White Star's Australian interests, represented by the *Ceramic* and the *Ionic*, were transferred to Shaw Savill & Albion, the premier shipping company operating to the Antipodes. Cunard's contribution to the combine was the express liners *Aquitania, Berengaria* and *Mauretania* and the twelve cabin liners, *Carinthia, Franconia, Laconia, Samaria, Scythia, Lancastria, Alaunia, Ascania, Aurania, Andania, Antonia* and *Ausonia*.

There is no doubt but that Cunard had the lion's share of the newer liners while White Star had some ageing vessels. With a glut of berths now available some of the older pre-war tonnage was disposed of. For a start the former Royal Mail liners *Albertic* and the *Calgaric*, both laid up the previous year, were sold. The *Albertic* was sold to Japanese shipbreakers in July for £34,000 and sailed the following month for Osaka. The *Calgaric* was sold to shipbreakers in Rosyth for £31,000 and left Pembroke on 20 December arriving at her final destination on Christmas Day.

It is interesting to note that the former Cunard ships in the Cunard White Star Line Limited wore the Cunard house-flag superior to that of its White Star partner whereas former White Star vessels wore the White Star pennant above the Cunard house-flag.

The *Majestic*, which was still the world's largest liner and the biggest in the combined fleet, had, in September, encountered a huge Atlantic wave which struck the liner and poured tons of water onto her upperworks. The Master, Captain Trant, was injured and the *Majestic*'s Staff Captain had to assume command for the remainder of the voyage. Later the same month she ran aground off Calshot, near the Bramble Bank in the

A fifty-ton electric gantry at work on the *Majestic* in the King George V Dock, Southampton. *Courtesy Stothert & Pitt Ltd*

Solent. The *Majestic* eventually refloated herself under her own power and without damage.

In the early hours of 24 September, while on a voyage from Liverpool to New York, the *Laconia* was in collision off Cape Cod with the US freighter *Pan Royal* of Wilmington, Delaware. The damage was superficial and both ships continued on their respective voyages.

The highlight of 1934 for the new company and a fillip for the whole nation was the launching of 534 as the *Queen Mary* on 26 September. She was launched in the

**After nineteen years service, the *Aquitania* underwent a three-month overhaul and refit during 1933. She was to last another seventeen years. *John Anderson***

**A record transatlantic passage of 5 days, 13 hours and 40 minutes was made by the *Aquitania* in June 1934. *Tom Rayner Collection***

The *Adriatic* seen here cruising from Liverpool on 25 May 1934, near the end of her career. *Tom Rayner Collection*

The *Laurentic* became a 'Holy' ship when she made a special cruise to Italy during Easter 1934. *Tom Rayner Collection*

presence of King George V and Queen Mary, the Queen herself performing the naming ceremony. At the time she was the first British liner to have been launched in the presence of a reigning king and queen and she was also the first to be named after a reigning queen. Her launching displacement was some 40,000 tons, a world record.

In the month following the *Queen Mary*'s launch the *Mauretania* was withdrawn from service. In the preceding year she had steamed 77,500 miles at an average speed of 25.5 knots. Towards the end of 1934 more of the older tonnage was sold off.

**The *Olympic* passing the Royal Yacht
Squadron, Cowes, during the mid-1930s**

**OPPOSITE: A picture of the *Olympic*
tendering either at Cherbourg or Cobh, prior
to her departure for New York. *Mrs P de
Kerbrech 'Master Detective' Collection***

The last and largest of White Star's original
Big Four, the *Adriatic*, was sold to Japanese
shipbreakers for £62,000.

On 13 December, while at New York, the
*Britannic* had a small fire in her fan space
but it was quickly brought under control.
While under the command of the famous
Cunard Master, James Bisset, the *Ascania*
sped to the assistance of the stricken tramp
steamer *Usworth* on 14 December. The
*Usworth* later sank in heavy seas off Nova
Scotia with a loss of fifteen lives.

Among the less newsworthy events for the
year, the *Berengaria* ran into a Force 9 gale

while on an eastbound crossing which made
her a day late arriving at Southampton.
However, she managed to make a record
turnround, spending only 15¾ hours in port
during which time a party of carpenters
worked all night to repair the storm damage.

Despite the pruned down combined fleet of
Cunard White Star and the reduction of
potential carrying berths, the Company
nevertheless carried a total of 118,269
passengers across the Atlantic for the year
ending 1934. This was not a statistic to be
particularly proud of but it marked a turning
point for the Company's fortunes as the

effects of the Depression eased. Passenger figures for the North Atlantic run generally bottomed-out in 1934 and thereafter each year showed a progressive improvement.

**ABOVE: Exit the *Ceramic* to Shaw Savill in 1934, following the merger.** *Tom Rayner Collection*

**... and also the *Ionic*.** *Tom Rayner Collection*

This imposing view shows the *Majestic*'s bridge. One can only imagine the height of the wave that she encountered in 1934. *John Anderson*

BELOW: While off Cape Cod, the *Laconia* was in collision with the *Pan Royal*. No serious damage was sustained by either vessel. *Tom Rayner Collection*

TOP: Laid up at Southampton – the *Mauretania*. *World Ship Photo Library*

On 14 December 1934 the *Ascania* went to the assistance of the stricken trampship *Usworth*. *John Clarkson, Hutton*

The *Olympic* (left) and *Mauretania* nearing departure, together in the Ocean Dock. Such was the scene at Southampton prior to the 1930s. *Southampton City Museums*

THE YEAR OPENED with the *Mauretania* still laid up and a slight scare when, in New York in January, the *Georgic* experienced a small fire in her cargo hold which delayed her sailing for some hours. This was quickly brought under control and it was discovered that negligible damage had been sustained.

Three months later the *Georgic*, along with the *Britannic*, was transferred to the London to New York service, their itinerary taking in Southampton, Le Havre, and Cobh outward and homeward. At the time they were the largest liners to use the Port of London. In order to place them on this route the *Franconia* and the *Carinthia* were displaced and switched to the Liverpool to New York run instead.

Following her final round trip, which commenced from Southampton on 27 March, the *Olympic* was withdrawn from service. From that point the *Majestic*, which remained on the run, maintained the express service along with the *Aquitania* and the *Berengaria*, which had by then replaced the *Mauretania*. This service was operated until the summer season.

During April the *Aquitania* operated on a cruise to the Mediterranean from Southampton. While returning to her home port on 11 April she went aground off Southampton in an attempt to dock in a 60mph gale. She was refloated after 26 hours with the aid of 10 tugs, and sustained no damage. In the same month the new French liner *Normandie* underwent sea trials in

The *Georgic* in the River Mersey on 2 June 1934. The following year she transferred to the London – New York service. *Tom Rayner Collection*

RIGHT: A strong gale forced the *Aquitania* aground at the entrance to Southampton Water on 11 April 1935. A battery of ten tugs, four of which are hidden behind the liner, assisted in freeing her. *Popperfoto*

which she averaged some 31.9 knots. A month later, on 20 May, the *Normandie* commenced her maiden voyage from Le Havre to New York via Southampton and on this trip she captured the Blue Riband in both directions from Italy's *Rex*. The modern 'superliner' of the mid-1930s had arrived and not only was she the fastest in the world but at 79,280 gross tons she was also the largest; the *Majestic* had lost her heavyweight crown, being displaced into second place.

The year 1935 also marked the Silver Jubilee of King George V and in May there was a naval review held at Spithead to mark the occasion. Among the vessels that represented the Merchant Navy were Cunard White Star's *Berengaria* and

*Homeric*. In addition there was the *Lancastria* which had made a special six-day cruise from Liverpool with spectators on board. These liners were among others forming a line on the seaward side of the line of warships and by comparison they dwarfed some of the largest battleships in attendance. It had been hoped that the *Mauretania*, then at Southampton preparing

for her departure to Rosyth where she was to be broken up, would be present at this royal event as a swan-song to her career, but she was not.

OPPOSITE: The *Lancastria* was present at King George V's Fleet Review in 1935. *Tom Rayner Collection*

In the June of 1935, she had been sold to Messrs Bolckow Vaughan, the shipbreakers, and on 1 July she left Southampton on her last voyage for Rosyth. She had served the Company well and had been a popular ship with all but she was now dated, of Edwardian vintage with no swimming pool or gymnasium and, having lost her speed records, she was considered to lack 'selling' power or, as we say nowadays, was 'unmarketable'. Her final departure was broadcast to the nation; however, for this trip she was a shadow of her former glory, her white-painted hull being rust-streaked and grimy. In addition, her masts had been cut down to enable her to pass under the Forth Bridge. A host of vessels blew their sirens in a farewell salute as she passed down Southampton Water, and all along the shore at Cowes and at Stokes Bay, Southsea and Ryde, crowds gathered to witness her passing. Cunard White Star had requested the local Isle of Wight ferry company, Red Funnel Steamers, to reserve the name *Mauretania* for them and the little paddle steamer *Queen* was renamed temporarily after the 'Grand Old Lady of the Atlantic'. The *Mauretania*'s vacant lay-up berth at Southampton was occupied by the *Olympic*.

On 18 August the *Laurentic*, which was still on her cruising itinerary, was outward bound from Liverpool to Northern Ports with 620 passengers on board when she collided with the Blue Star liner *Napier Star*. The accident occurred in the Irish Sea in the early hours of the morning in foggy weather. Six members of the *Napier Star*'s crew were killed and another four injured in the collision. The Blue Star ship tore a great hole in the starboard bow of the *Laurentic* and in so doing smashed twelve of the crew's cabins in the forecastle head. Although passengers were ordered to don lifejackets no panic ensued and there was no danger of her sinking. The *Laurentic* returned to Liverpool where the passengers who were booked on the cruise were transferred to the *Lancastria* and the *Homeric*.

Ironically, on 5 September, the *Laurentic*'s sister-ship, the *Doric*, which had been employed on tourist cruises out of Southampton at a minimum rate of £12 for thirteen days afloat, was also in a collision

A lone piper plays a lament as the *Mauretania* reaches her final destination at Rosyth. *Authors' Collection*

with the French vessel *Formigny*, also in fog off Finnisterre. She put into Vigo in Northern Spain for temporary repairs which included the fitting of a cofferdam. She then returned to the United Kingdom whereupon she was immediately sold for breaking up at Newport, Monmouthshire.

Earlier, on 20 August, the *Olympic*, which by then had been laid up at Southampton for five months, was opened for inspection to prospective buyers. At that time she was the largest vessel ever to be offered for scrap value. Later, on 10 September, Sir John Jervis bought her for £100,000 only to resell her to Thomas W Ward & Co Ltd for the same amount with the provision that she be broken up at Jarrow to alleviate the chronic

unemployment situation in that area. Her passing saw the Big Six reduced to four.

The next day, 11 September, the *Berengaria* left Southampton for New York after a record turnround of 13¼ hours in port. During that half day more than 1000 passengers and their baggage were dealt with and in addition over 4000 bags of mail were transferred. She also bunkered 7000 tons of fuel oil and took on one million gallons of fresh water. The ship's stores were victualled with 30 tons of provisions.

As to the *Homeric*, which had been used almost exclusively for cruising since 1932 and which recently had been present at the Naval Review, she returned to Southampton on 25 September after a successful cruise which was to be her last. Her cruise programme was taken over by the *Franconia* with effect from 28 September and the

*Homeric* was laid up off Ryde, Isle of Wight for the winter, awaiting disposal.

October proved a black month for former White Star tonnage, for the Old Reliable, as the *Olympic* had been dubbed during her wartime days, left Southampton for Jarrow-on-Tyne for the breakers. The Company and an Admiralty Court convened an enquiry into the collision between the *Laurentic* and the *Napier Star* three months before. Their findings were that both vessels were equally to blame for the collision; later, in December, the *Laurentic* was laid up. Though it was not realised at the time, this more or less marked the end of the *Laurentic*'s civilian passenger-carrying career.

The Silver Jubilee celebrations and Naval Review for that year gave a great boost to the North Atlantic trade and the total number of passengers that crossed that year was almost 500,000. Despite the lay-up of some liners and the parade of others to the breaker's yard, the passenger receipts for Cunard White Star were 134,362, almost double that of their nearest rival, North German Lloyd – an encouraging sign.

93

# CHAPTER 9

# 1936 — THE ZENITH

THE YEAR 1936 marked the end for three more of the former White Star vessels but, with the balance more than restored, it also witnessed the entry into service of the *Queen Mary*. January opened with the *Carinthia* being transferred to the New York to West Indies service.

The *Majestic*'s last voyage took place from Southampton to New York on 13 February and upon her return she was laid up at Southampton. Ironically, on the previous day, the *Homeric*, which had been laid up off Clyde, was offered for sale and later, on 27 February, she was sold to Thomas W Ward of Sheffield for about £75,000, sailing for Inverkeithing to be broken up in March. It had been rumoured that her former owners North German Lloyd were interested in purchasing her as a consort to her near

sister, the *Columbus*, thereby achieving what World War I had prevented. The speculation was scotched by her sale for demolition.

The almost-completed *Queen Mary*, the symbol of renaissance for the nation after the lean years of the Depression, was to be classed as a Cabin ship by the North Atlantic Conference and the intention was for her to run the express service along with the *Aquitania* and *Berengaria*. After leaving her birthplace on the Clyde on 26 March she arrived at Southampton the following day for drydocking in preparation for her speed trials. As she was eased up past the New Docks to enter the King George V Graving Dock, the *Queen Mary* passed the former heavyweight *Majestic* which was dressed overall in salute to her successor. It also seemed to be in recognition that her days as a liner were over while the *Queen Mary*'s were only just about to begin. On 15 April the *Queen Mary* left Southampton for her speed trials off the Isle of Arran with over

**The *Queen Mary* leaving the fitting out basin at John Brown's yard on 24 March 1936.** *The University Archives, The University of Liverpool*

1000 people on board. The actual trials took place four days later and, although at the time no official figures were issued, Cunard White Star and John Brown announced their complete satisfaction with her performance. An unofficial estimate put her maximum speed achieved at 32.84 knots.

Following her trials the *Queen Mary* returned to Southampton on 20 April where she was berthed at the Ocean Dock to take on stores for her shake-down cruise. The massive vessel was insured for £4.8 million of which £3 million was placed in the open market and the remainder was underwritten by the British government. A month later, on 14 May, she left Southampton for a day's cruise with a large party of distinguished guests on board. Two days later, back in port again, a large delegation of MPs made a tour

The *Queen Mary* departs on her maiden
voyage. *Authors' Collection*

of inspection and had lunch aboard, and on
25 May, the new monarch, King Edward
VIII, Queen Mary the Queen Mother, the
Duke and Duchess of York, the Duke and
Duchess of Kent, the Duchess of Gloucester
and Princess Elizabeth also visited the liner
to inspect her.

Finally, two days later, on 27 May 1936, the
*Queen Mary* embarked on her maiden voyage
to New York. She left Southampton at
4.30pm to a tumultuous send-off from
thousands of spectators lining the quays and
vantage points all along the Solent. After
picking up passengers at Cherbourg she set
out across the Atlantic. She made this

The *Queen Mary*'s departure on her maiden
voyage on 27 May 1936. Alongside at 46
berth is the *Georgic* while behind at 22 berth
is Royal Mail's *Arlanza. Les Smith Collection
courtesy of Bert Moody*

westbound crossing at an average speed of 29.133 knots and reached the Ambrose Light Vessel, the end of the passage, 4 days, 12 hours and 24 minutes after clearing the breakwater at Cherbourg. Her arrival in New York harbour on 1 June was accompanied by the sort of reception that only that city can give – blimps, aircraft, tug-boats spraying huge jets of water into the air and endless small craft all hailing Great Britain's wonder ship in a mass throng!

The age of the super liner had finally arrived for Britain. At 80,773 gross tons the *Queen Mary* was the world's largest liner and pushed the *Normandie*, albeit temporarily, into second place. On the return leg of her maiden voyage, the *Queen Mary* arrived at Southampton on 10 June after making the passage from the Ambrose Light Vessel to Cherbourg in 4 days, 15 hours and 16 minutes at an average speed of 28.74 knots.

With all the hullabaloo surrounding the *Queen Mary*'s entry into service, these events rather overshadowed the *Majestic*'s disposal. After three months of lay-up at Southampton she was sold for scrap to Thomas W Ward for £115,000. Subsequently, she was stripped of most of her external fittings and her masts and three funnels were cut down to facilitate her passage under the Forth Railway Bridge to the breaker's yard at Inverkeithing.

Around this time the Admiralty Board had decided that a training facility for new entry Boy Seamen and Artificer Apprentices should be sited at Rosyth in Scotland. As a shore establishment would take some time to build, they were looking around for a stop-gap measure. The huge *Majestic* was ideal for a floating training establishment because she could accommodate the proposed 2000 new entries and the Admiralty decided to acquire her. It is believed that the Royal Navy could not buy the liner, even at her scrap price, so an exchange deal was proposed. The Royal Navy would trade for the liner twenty-four old warships whose total tonnage was

equivalent to that of the *Majestic*. The exchange was agreed and the *Majestic* became the property of the Royal Navy following which she was taken in hand by John I Thornycroft for extensive alterations.

As for the *Queen Mary*, after her running-in period she arrived in New York on 25 August after making the fastest westbound crossing of the Atlantic to date. The voyage took 4 days, 7 hours and 12 minutes at an average speed of 30.01 knots so gaining for herself the Blue Riband. She arrived back at Southampton on 31 August after a record eastbound passage of 3 days, 23 hours and 57 minutes at an average speed of 30.63 knots. Thus she recaptured the title for Great Britain barely seven years after it had been conceded to Continental rivals. Although the congratulatory messages poured in to the ship's Master, Captain Edgar Britten, from all directions, the Cunard White Star Line said they would not accept the Hales Trophy presented by Member of Parliament H K Hales as a physical representation of the Blue Riband, and which was then held by the French Line. The directors were of the opinion that a trophy presented for international competition introduced an undesirable element into the operation of big ships.

How they could have reached this decision when they already possessed the world's fastest ship and what the undesirable element was is beyond the authors' comprehension. Perhaps it amounted to no more than another example of the tongue-in-cheek modesty that is so typical of the British when they achieve great things.

In September, the *Laurentic*, which had been laid up at Southampton since December 1935, was commissioned as a troopship for the transportation of troops to Palestine (now Israel) to help augment the Palestine Police in the mandated territory. Her original accommodation for 600 Cabin, 400 Tourist and 500 Third Class passengers was stripped and on 14 September she left Southampton on her first voyage in her new role.

With the *Queen Mary* an unqualified success, the Cunard White Star Line placed an order

After three months' lay-up at Southampton, the *Majestic* was sold at £115,000 for scrap. This aerial view shows that most of her lifeboats have been removed. *Brocklesby Collection - Southampton City Museums*

The *Majestic*'s former elegant Pompeian swimming pool became the baths on board HMS *Caledonia*. It was one of the luxury fittings retained from her liner days. *HMS Sultan Museum*

The *Queen Mary* passing Calshot on 31 August 1936 after gaining the Blue Riband at an average speed of over 30 knots. Three Red Funnel paddle steamers escort the record breaker up Southampton Water. *C Konings*

for a second great ship with John Brown that October, in pursuance of their plans for a two-ship express service. Other shipbuilders had tendered for the contract, among them Cammell Laird on the Mersey and a Tyneside consortium of Swan Hunter and Vickers-Armstrong, but the Clydebank yard's advantage of experience gained with the *Queen Mary* beat off the other competitors. So the keel of yard number 552 was laid in December 1936 with her entry into service scheduled for 1940, Cunard's centenary year.

On 20 October, while undergoing an overhaul at Southampton, the *Berengaria*, the last of the HAPAG trio to remain in passenger service, received extensive though localised damage when fire swept through several of her cabins. She was, however, ready in time to resume her North Atlantic timetable, sailing on 18 November when she relieved the *Aquitania* on the New York service via Cherbourg, continuing through the winter in consort with the *Queen Mary*. Prior to the winter months she had run in conjunction with both the *Aquitania* and the *Queen Mary* on this service. The three liners had maintained the twice-weekly sailings from Southampton and New York setting a standard of regularity and excellence that the other companies had difficulty in matching. Indeed, during the year the *Aquitania* even made her best run to date, crossing from Cherbourg to the Ambrose light vessel in 5 days, 10 hours and 6 minutes at an average speed of 24.82 knots.

B Y 1937, CUNARD WHITE Star's plans for the future Atlantic service looked like coming to fruition in all respects. As part of the fleet rejuvenation four of the Big Six had been sold: the *Mauretania*. *Olympic* and *Homeric* for scrap while the *Majestic* had been refitted by John I

Thornycroft of Southampton and converted into the training ship HMS *Caledonia*. This had been achieved by 2000 shipyard employees who had worked thirteen hours a day, seven days a week, for almost eight months. The cost of the conversion to the Royal Navy was estimated to be £472,000. The great ship left

Southampton for Rosyth on 8 April and later, on 23 April, she was officially commissioned as HMS *Caledonia*. As such she was the Royal Navy's largest warship on active service.

With these four liners gone, the vacuum created by their withdrawal was to be filled

A tranquil waterside view of HMS *Caledonia*. **HMS Sultan Museum**

by the 80,000 tonners *Queen Mary* and yard number 552. However, it was apparent that a third ship of smaller size would be required to maintain the service in winter when one or other of the larger vessels was undergoing an annual overhaul, also in cases of emergency. So it was that an intermediate liner of 35,700 gross tons was laid down at Cammell Laird's Birkenhead yard on 24 May 1937. She was to take the name *Mauretania* but unlike her famous namesake the new liner was not intended to break records. Instead, it was planned that she would run in consort with the *Georgic* and *Britannic* on the London to New York intermediate service. Nevertheless, she would also be required to give a sufficient turn of speed to substitute for the *Queen Mary* and her sister on the express service.

At that time the Merchant Shipping Act did not encourage the duplication of names for vessels on the British registry. As has already been mentioned, to overcome the problem Cunard White Star had taken the initiative of coming to an agreement with

Red Funnel Steamers, the company operating a ferry service between Southampton and the Isle of Wight, whereby their paddle steamer *Queen* would be renamed *Mauretania*, albeit temporarily. Thus, the famous name *Mauretania* was reserved until the new intermediate liner was ready to claim it.

Following the abdication of King Edward VIII and the accession to the throne of the Duke of York to become King George VI, another naval review took place at Spithead on 20 May 1937, to celebrate the Coronation. Changes in naval trends since the Jubilee review of two years previous were evident. Eleven fewer battleships were present than before while the number of aircraft carriers had increased to five. Cunard White Star were represented by the *Aquitania* and the *Laurentic* though only in an unofficial capacity, carrying sightseers to view the event.

By the end of 1937 the *Queen Mary* had settled down on her New York shuttle service and, like her French rival *Normandie*, which had regained the Blue Riband honours that year, she was booked to capacity trip after trip. The *Queen Mary* had carried a larger number of passengers on

each round voyage than any other liner on the route that season, while the other giants of the North Atlantic, the *Aquitania*, *Bremen*, *Empress of Britain* and *Ile de France* were almost as popular. The smaller Cabin vessels like the *Georgic*, French Lines' *Champlain* and United States Lines' *Manhattan* as well as their consorts also carried their full quota and the number of passengers passing through Southampton in 1937 was a record for the port.

Once again, during April, the 23-year-old *Aquitania* managed another record westbound passage from Cherbourg to

... and also for the *Georgic* which averaged
745 passengers over sixteen crossings. *John
Clarkson, Hutton*

The *Berengaria* arrived back at Southampton without passengers in March 1938. By contrast, during 1937 she had carried a total of 21,766. She is seen here with Imperial Airways flying boats at their terminal. *Pamlin Prints*

The *Laurentic* laid up at Southampton in 1937, following her trooping trip to Palestine. The parade is thought to be during 'Merchant Navy Week', 17–24 July, a popular event up until 1939. *Southampton City Museums*

Ambrose Light Vessel. She achieved a new personal best time for the crossing of 5 days, 8 hours and 37 minutes at an average speed of 24.87 knots – what a fitting tribute this was to the high standards of British marine engineering of those days.

A setback for Cunard White Star heralded 1938 for, on 3 March, while the *Berengaria* was berthed at New York, a fire swept through her Main Lounge and, although it was quickly put out, the United States' authorities refused clearance for passengers to embark for her next voyage on the grounds that she was a fire risk. So the *Berengaria* sailed for Southampton via Cherbourg empty apart from the mails. It was to be her last commercial voyage. Upon her arrival at Southampton she was surveyed and then laid up for the remainder of the season. That October she was sold to shipbreakers – the last of Albert Ballin's original HAPAG trio to be withdrawn from service and also the oldest.

Simultaneously, the Company's revival received a terrific boost for on 28 July the new *Mauretania* was launched from the Cammell Laird yard. During the ceremony a telegram was received from the Master and crew of the small paddle steamer *Corfe Castle*, the former *Queen*, which had adopted

The new *Mauretania*, following her launch from Cammel Laird's yard, Birkenhead.
*John Clarkson, Hutton*

**The Red Funnel paddle steamer *Queen* bearing the famous name *Mauretania*.**
***Pamlin Prints***

the name *Mauretania* to preserve it pending the construction of the new Cunard liner. The message read: 'On the day of your baptism your diminutive step-sister sends greetings and cordial good wishes for a long and famous career.'

The following month, on 4 August, the *Queen Mary* commenced her fastest ever westbound voyage. She crossed from Bishop Rock to the Ambrose Light Vessel in 3 days, 21 hours and 48 minutes at an average speed of 30.99 knots. On her return voyage, departing New York on 10 August, she made her fastest eastbound passage taking 3 days, 20 hours and 42 minutes from Ambrose Light Vessel to Bishop Rock at an average speed of 31.69 knots. These performances secured the Atlantic Blue Riband for the *Queen Mary* for the next fourteen years.

On 28 September 1938 the *Queen Mary*'s partner, the *Queen Elizabeth*, was launched by Her Majesty Queen Elizabeth (later Her Royal Highness the Queen Mother), the largest liner ever to be built in the world. She entered the waters of the Clyde in the presence of more than a quarter of a million spectators. She was scheduled to enter

service in March 1940 but the storm clouds of war were already gathering over Europe and the plans for a two-ship express service were destined to be postponed, though this was not realised at the time. In fact, the Munich crisis of that year led to unsettled business and tourist conditions in Europe generally, which in turn had an adverse effect on Atlantic traffic. This was reflected in a distinct fall-off in passenger numbers compared with 1937.

ABSTRACT OF LOG OF THE

# CUNARD WHITE STAR R.M.S. "QUEEN MARY"

COMMODORE R. B. IRVING, O.B.E., R.D., R.N.R.

SOUTHAMPTON AND CHERBOURG TO NEW YORK.

| Date (1938) | Dist. | Latitude N. | Longitude W. | Weather, etc. |
|---|---|---|---|---|
| Wed., August 3 | | | | At 6.00 p.m. (B.S.T.) Left Berth, Southampton<br>At 10.04 p.m. (B.S.T.) Arrived Cherbourg |
| ,, ,, ,,<br>Thursday, ,, 4 | | | | At 2.24 a.m. (B.S.T.) Left Cherbourg |
| ,, ,, ,, | 322 | 49.55 | 9.52 | Strong breeze, rough sea, misty patches<br>Speed reduced 1 hr., 26 mins. |
| Friday, ,, 5 | 759 | 48.50 | 29.13 | Mod. breeze, slight sea, overcast, dull to clear |
| Saturday, ,, 6 | 790 | 44.06 | 46.55 | Light breeze, slight sea, cloudy and clear |
| Sunday, ,, 7 | 784 | 41.17 | 64.05 | Gentle breeze, slight sea, cloudy, rain showers |
| Monday, ,, 8 | 442 | To Ambrose | Chan. L.V. | At 1.30 a.m. (E.D.S.T.) Ambrose Channel L.V.<br>abeam |
| Total | 3,097 | nautical miles | | |

**Passage Cherbourg to Ambrose C.L.V.:**
**4 days, 4 hours, 6 minutes**
**Average speed: 30.94 knots**

**Passage Bishop's R. to Ambrose C.L.V.:**
**3 days, 21 hours, 48 minutes**
**Average speed: 30.99 knots**

ABSTRACT OF LOG OF THE

# CUNARD WHITE STAR R.M.S. "QUEEN MARY"

COMMODORE R. B. IRVING, O.B.E., R.D., R.N.R.

### SOUTHAMPTON AND CHERBOURG TO NEW YORK.

| Date (1939) | Dist. | Latitude | Longitude | Weather, etc. |
|---|---|---|---|---|
| | | N. | W. | |
| Wed'day, June 14 | | | | At 10.16 a.m. (B.S.T.) Left Berth, Southampton |
| ,, ,, ,, | | | | At 2.32 p.m. (B.S.T.) Arrived Cherbourg |
| ,, ,, ,, | | | | At 5.00 p.m. (B.S.T.) Left Cherbourg |
| Thursday, ,, 15 | 566 | 49.18 | 16.04 | Moderate wind and sea, mod. swell, o'cast, rain |
| Friday, ,, 16 | 717 | 45.53 | 33.04 | Fresh breeze, rough sea, mod. swell, cloudy |
| Saturday, ,, 17 | 714 | 40.30 | 47.33 | Fresh to strong winds, rough sea, mod. swell |
| Sunday, ,, 18 | 714 | 40.37 | 63.12 | Moderate variable winds, cloudy and clear |
| Monday, ,, 19 | 484 | To Ambrose | Chan. L.V. | At 5.13 a.m. (E.D.S.T.) Ambrose Channel L.V. abeam |
| Total | 3,195 | nautical miles | | |

PASSAGE—4 days, 17 hours, 13 minutes.     AVERAGE SPEED—28.22 knots.

# CHAPTER 11

# 1939 — A FAMOUS NAME REVIVED

THE NEXT YEAR, 1939, the new *Mauretania* sailed on her maiden voyage. She left Liverpool bound for New York on 17 June 1939, arriving back at Southampton via Cherbourg on 7 July. On 6 August she visited London, the largest liner ever to enter the port. The 2¾ mile passage on 'stand-by' from Tilbury to the King George V Dock was described as one of the finest pilotage feats ever carried out on the River Thames.

In passing, it is of interest to note that the *Mauretania* had fitted aboard her a small portion of the interior panelling from her illustrious predecessor scrapped some five years earlier.

The following month, on 1 September, Britain declared war on Germany. For safety reasons the boys and apprentices were moved ashore from HMS *Caledonia*, the former *Majestic*, on 2 September. She was considered a hazard to the dockside because of her size, especially if she was to be bombed. So it was, during the same month, that she was towed out of her basin to a point west of the Forth Railway Bridge and a good distance away from the main shipping channel. She then had water pumped into her bilges so that she settled on an even keel on the bottom of the Forth. This precaution was taken in case of air raids so that she could not break adrift and obstruct the seaway to Rosyth. Any thoughts of seriously considering her for use as a troopship were forestalled on 29 September when she caught fire and was gutted. The fire rendered her useless for Royal Navy purposes and in the spring of 1940 she was sold back to Thomas W Ward who began the job of salvaging the remains of the old liner in October 1942. The *Caledonia* was demolished down to the waterline to lighten her and, in July 1943, the remainder of her hull was raised and towed to Inverkeithing where scrapping was completed. In a sense she was just outlived by her younger sister for scrapping of the *Berengaria* was not completed until 1946.

Thus the ex-*Majestic* was denied to the Ministry of War Transport although the two *Queens* which had in part displaced her more than compensated for the lost capacity that the *Majestic* could have offered.

So from peacetime roles the ships of the Cunard White Star fleet were called up and requisitioned for government service, for the *Aquitania* for the second time during her career. Some, like the *Andania, Carinthia* and *Laconia* did not survive the war. Particularly poignant was the loss of the *Lancastria*, sunk while embarking 9000 British troops at St Nazaire with terrific loss of life. Others, like the *Antonia, Ausonia* and *Aurania* were sold to the Admiralty never to return to their former commercial roles. The *Georgic* survived the war but returned only as a shadow of her former luxury following a fire at Port Tewfik in 1941. She was rebuilt to serve only as a utility vessel until the end of her days in 1956.

**Two views of the new *Mauretania* manoeuvring in the River Mersey in preparation for her maiden voyage from Liverpool on 17 June 1939. *Tom Rayner Collection***

A close shave. The *Mauretania* entering the King George V Dock, London, in August 1939, after her maiden crossing of the Atlantic. With World War II less than a month away, this may be one of the last pre-war photos of her. *The Museum of London*

The *Queen Elizabeth* crossed the Atlantic on her maiden voyage on 26 February 1940 in complete secrecy. Together, the *Queen Elizabeth* and *Queen Mary* were to distinguish themselves during the War by their exploits as troop transports. Between them they carried 1,622,054 troops during their six years of military service.

Our story concludes with the final act involving Cunard White Star in the 1930s – the *Mauretania* departing from Liverpool on 10 December 1939 bound for New York where she was to be converted for troop carrying purposes.

The decade had come to an end on a lower

A night-time photo of HMS *Caledonia*. She must have proved an expensive vessel to run for she was capable of supplying her own electric power; fresh water however was pumped aboard. 1939 meant the lights going out all over Europe, and also going out permanently for the famous ex-liner. *HMS Sultan Museum*

HMS *Caledonia* dressed overall *c* 1939. A serious fire that year prevented her use as a troopship against the country in which she was built. *HMS Sultan Museum*

OPPOSITE: Steaming through the Gaillard Cut of the Panama Canal, the *Mauretania* is in her wartime livery. *Authors' collection*

The *Lancastria* was sunk with terrific loss of life. *John Clarkson, Hutton*

note than that on which it had opened. For six years the lights went out over Europe, the Atlantic and the whole world. Throughout, the ships of Cunard White Star played their part in the support of the forces of freedom, truth and democracy. When peace returned in 1945 and the pieces of the shattered Atlantic services were picked up it heralded a period of unprecedented prosperity for the Cunard White Star Line, a prosperity largely due to the momentous events of the 1930s and the major rebuilding programme that was launched during that era.

The liners get called up. Here the *Aquitania* is seen in wartime grey for the second time in her career. *L L von Münching*

OPPOSITE: Requiem for a heavyweight. The end of the *Majestic*, seen here in 1943 in a partially scrapped state. It is reported that her scrapping provided nearly 40,000 tons of first class steel for the Second World War effort. *Imperial War Museum*

The *Queen Mary* sports her degaussing cable. *World Ship Photo Library*

The *Queen Elizabeth*, the world's largest liner. A new Cunarder for a new decade. She did not enter commercial service until 1946. Here she is seen in wartime grey and 'silent running'. *C Konings*

Fleet List of All Major Passenger Lines Owned by Cunard, White Star and
Cunard White Star Lines During the 1930s

*List of abbreviations used in technical terminology:*

Motor

| | |
|---|---|
| 4SC DA | *Four-stroke cycle, Double Acting* |
| bhp | *Brake horsepower* |

Steam

| | |
|---|---|
| ihp | *Indicated horsepower* |
| shp | *Shaft horsepower* |
| LP | *Low Pressure* |
| DR | *Double Reduction* |
| SR | *Single Reduction* |

NB All technical data is in Imperial units.

*Key*

**Name** (period with Company). Shipbuilder. Date
delivered. Gross tonnage. Length overall × breadth
(in feet). Type of machinery. Horsepower. Service
speed. Number of passengers by class (where known
for the 1930s). Fate.

Note: Where applicable the previous names and/or
the future names of the ship appear after its name as
a Cunard, White Star or Cunard White Star ship.

## Cunard Steamship Co

*Caronia* (1905–1932). John Brown & Co. Ltd,
Glasgow. 2/1905. 19,594 grt. 678 × 72.2ft. Twin
quadruple expansion steam engines. 22,000ihp. 18
knots. Passengers 425 Cabin, 365 Tourist, 650
Third. Scrapped at Osaka from 1933 under the name
*Taiseiyo Maru*.

*Carmania* (1905–1932). John Brown & Co. Ltd,
Glasgow. 11/1905. 19,524 grt. 675 × 72.2ft. Three
steam turbines directly coupled to 3 shafts.
21,000shp. 18 knots. Passengers 425 Cabin, 365
Tourist, 650 Third. Scrapped at Blyth from 1933.

*Mauretania* (1907–1935). Swan Hunter &
Wigham Richardson, Wallsend. 11/1907.
30,696grt. 790×88ft. Four steam turbines directly
coupled to 4 shafts. 65,000 shp. 25 knots.
Passengers 589 First, 400 Second, 767 Third.
Scrapped at Rosyth from 1935.

*Aquitania* (1914–1949). John Brown & Co. Ltd,
Glasgow. 5/1914. 45,647grt. 901 × 97.1ft. Four
steam turbines directly coupled to 4 shafts.

60,000shp. 23 knots. Passengers 618 First, 614
Second, 1998 Third. Scrapped at Faslane from 1950.

*Berengaria* (1921–1938). ex *Imperator*
(Hamburg America Line). AG Vulcan, Hamburg.
4/1913. 52,226grt; 909 × 98.1ft. Four steam
turbines directly coupled to 4 shafts. 56,000 shp. 23
knots. Passengers 972 First, 630 Second, 505
Tourist, 606 Third. Scrapped at Jarrow, later
Rosyth, from 1938.

*Albania* (1921–1930). *California* (Libera
Triestina) 1930. Scott's, Greenock. 12/1920.
12,768grt; 539×64ft. Steam turbines SR geared to
2 shafts. 6800shp. 13 knots. Passengers 480 Cabin.
Sunk by air-launched torpedo off Syracuse, 11
August 1941.

*Scythia* (1921–1957). Vickers Ltd, Barrow-in-
Furness. 8/1921. 19,730grt. 624×73.5ft. Six steam
turbines DR geared to 2 shafts. 12,500shp. 16 knots.
Passengers 337 Cabin, 331 Tourist, 1100 Third.
Scrapped at Inverkeithing from 1958.

*Samaria* (1922–1955). Cammell Laird & Co. Ltd,
Birkenhead. 8/1921. 19,602grt. 624 × 73.5ft. Six
steam turbines DR geared to 2 shafts. 12,500 shp. 16
knots. Passengers 350 Cabin, 340 Tourist, 1100
Third. Scrapped at Inverkeithing from 1956.

*Laconia* (1922–1942). Swan Hunter & Wigham
Richardson, Newcastle. 1/1922. 19,680grt; 623 ×
73.2ft. Six steam turbines DR geared to 2 shafts.
12,500shp. 16 knots. Passengers 340 Cabin, 340
Tourist, 1100 Third. Torpedoed and sunk by U156
in the South Atlantic, 12 September 1942.

*Franconia* (1923–1956). John Brown & Co. Ltd,
Glasgow. 6/1923. 20,158grt. 623×73.2ft. Six steam
turbines DR geared to 2 shafts. 12,500shp. 16 knots.
Passengers: 240 Cabin, 460 Tourist, 950 Third.
Scrapped at Inverkeithing from 1956.

*Carinthia* (1925–1940). Vickers Ltd, Barrow-in-
Furness. 8/1925. 20,277grt. 624×73.5ft. Six steam
turbines DR geared to 2 shafts. 12,500shp. 16 knots.
Passengers 240 Cabin, 460 Tourist, 950 Third.
Torpedoed and sunk by U46 off the Irish coast, 6
June 1940.

*Lancastria* (1922–1940). ex *Tyrrhenia* (1924);
Wm Beardmore & Co., Glasgow. 12/1922.

16,243grt; 578 × 70.2ft. Six steam turbines DR
geared to 2 shafts. 12,500shp. 16 knots. Passengers
580 Cabin, 1000 Third. Bombed and sunk at St
Nazaire, 17 June 1940.

*Antonia* (1922–1942). HMS *Weyland*
(Admiralty) 1944. Vickers Ltd, Barrow-in-Furness.
6/1922. 13,867grt. 540 × 65.2ft. Four steam
turbines DR geared to 2 shafts. 8500shp. 14 knots.
Passengers 400 Cabin, 1000 Third. Scrapped in
Scotland from 1948.

*Ausonia* (1922–1942). HMS *Ausonia*
(Admiralty) 1942. W G Armstrong Whitworth &
Co., Newcastle. 6/1922. 13,912grt. 538 × 65.3ft.
Four steam turbines DR geared to 2 shafts. 8500shp.
14 knots. Passengers 400 Cabin, 1000 Third.
Scrapped at Castellon from 1965.

*Andania* (1922–1940). Hawthorn Leslie & Co.
Ltd, Hebburn-on-Tyne. 5/1922. 13,950grt. 538 ×
65.3ft. Four steam turbines DR geared to 2 shafts.
8500shp. 14 knots. Passengers 400 Cabin, 1000
Third. Torpedoed and sunk by UA70 near Iceland,
16 June 1940.

*Ascania* (1925–1956); W G Armstrong Whitworth & Co., Newcastle. 5/1925. 14,013grt. 538 ×
65.3ft. Four steam turbines DR geared to 2 shafts.
8500shp. 14 knots. Passengers 500 Cabin, 1200
Third. Scrapped at Newport, Monmouth, from
1957.

*Aurania* (1924–1942). HMS *Artifex* (Admiralty)
1944. Swan Hunter & Wigham Richardson,
Newcastle. 9/1924. 13,984grt. 540 × 65.2ft. Four
steam turbines DR geared to 2 shafts. 8500shp. 14
knots. Passengers 500 Cabin, 1200 Third. Scrapped
at La Spezia from 1961.

*Alaunia* (1925–1944). HMS *Alaunia*
(Admiralty) 1944. John Brown & Co. Ltd, Glasgow.
7/1925. 14,030grt. 538 × 65.3ft. Four steam
turbines DR geared to 2 shafts. 8500shp. 14 knots.
Passengers 484 Cabin, 1222 Third. Scrapped at
Blyth from 1957.

# White Star Line

***Corinthic*** (1902–1931). Harland & Wolff, Belfast. 7/1902. 12,231grt. 516 × 63.3ft. Twin quadruple expansion steam engines. 4400ihp. 13 knots. Passengers 121 First, 117 Second; 450 Third. Scrapped at Wallsend 1932.

***Ionic*** (1902–1934). Harland & Wolff, Belfast. 12/1902. 12,232grt. 516 × 63.3ft. Twin quadruple expansion steam engines. 4,400ihp. 13 knots. Passengers 238 Cabin, 450 Third. Transferred to Shaw Savill & Albion, 1934. Scrapped at Osaka from 1937.

***Cedric*** (1903–1931). Harland & Wolff, Belfast. 1/1903. 21,035grt. 700 × 75.3ft. Twin quadruple expansion steam engines. 12,600ihp. 16 knots. Passengers 347 Cabin, 250 Tourist, 1000 Third. Scrapped at Inverkeithing from 1932.

***Baltic*** (1904–1933). Harland & Wolff, Belfast. 6/1904. 23,884grt. 726 × 75.5ft. Twin quadruple expansion steam engines. 14,000ihp. 16 knots. Passengers 393 Cabin, 339 Tourist, 1150 Third. Scrapped at Osaka from 1933.

***Adriatic*** (1907–1934). Harland & Wolff, Belfast. 4/1907. 24,541grt. 726 × 75.6ft. Twin quadruple expansion steam engines. 16,000ihp. 17 knots. Passengers 506 Cabin, 560 Tourist, 404 Third. Scrapped at Osaka from 1935.

***Megantic*** (1909–1933). ex ***Albany***. Harland & Wolff, Belfast. 6/1909. 14,878grt. 565 × 67.5ft. Twin quadruple expansion steam engines. 11,000ihp. 16 knots. Passengers 452 Cabin, 260 Second, 550 Third. Scrapped at Osaka from 1933.

***Olympic*** (1911–1935). Harland & Wolff, Belfast. 5/1911. 46,439grt. 882 × 92.5ft. Twin triple expansion steam engines plus LP turbine. 51,000ihp (combined). 21.5 knots. Passengers 618 First, 447 Tourist, 382 Third. Scrapped at Jarrow, later Inverkeithing, from 1935.

***Ceramic*** (1913–1934). Harland & Wolff, Belfast. 7/1913. 18,481grt. 679 × 69.4ft. Twin triple expansion steam engines plus LP turbine. 9000ihp (combined). 15 knots. Passengers 820 Cabin. Transferred to Shaw Savill & Albion, 1934. Torpedoed and sunk by U515 off the Azores, 23 November 1942.

***Arabic*** (1921–1931). ex ***Berlin*** (North German Lloyd). AG Weser, Bremen. 4/1909. 16,786grt. 613 × 69.8ft. Twin quadruple expansion steam engines. 16,000ihp. 17 knots. Passengers 500 Cabin, 1200 Third. Chartered to Red Star Line 1926–1930. Scrapped at Genoa from 1932.

***Homeric*** (1922–1935). ex ***Columbus*** (North German Lloyd). F Schichau, Danzig. 1/1922. 34,351grt. 774 × 82.3ft. Twin triple expansion steam engines. 32,000ihp. 18 knots. Passengers 523 First, 841 Tourist, 314 Third. Scrapped at Inverkeithing from 1936.

***Majestic*** (1922–1936). ex ***Bismarck*** (Hamburg America Line). HMS ***Caledonia*** (Admiralty) 1936. Blohm & Voss, Hamburg. 3/1922. 56,551grt; 956 × 100ft. Four steam turbines directly coupled to 4 shafts. 80,000shp. 23 knots. Passengers 700 First, 545 Tourist, 850 Third. Burnt out and sunk at Rosyth, 29 September 1939. Scrapped from 1940 in situ.

***Doric*** (1923–1935). Harland & Wolff, Belfast. 5/1923. 16,484grt. 601 × 67.6ft. Two steam turbines SR geared to 2 shafts. 9000shp. 15 knots. Passengers 320 Cabin, 657 Tourist, 537 Third. Scrapped at Newport, Monmouth, from 1935 following a collision off Cape Finisterre.

***Albertic*** (1927–1934). ex ***Ohio*** (Royal Mail Line). ex ***München*** (North German Lloyd). AG Weser, Bremen. 3/1923. 18,940grt. 615 × 71.5ft. Twin quadruple expansion steam engines. 16,000ihp. 16 knots. Passengers 580 Cabin, 1700 Third. Scrapped at Osaka from 1935.

***Calgaric*** (1927–1933). ex ***Orca*** (Pacific Steam Navigation Co.). Harland & Wolff, Belfast. 5/1918 (cargo only). 12/1922. 16,063grt. 574 × 67.3ft. Twin triple expansion steam engines plus LP turbine. 11,900ihp (combined). 14 knots. Passengers 190 First, 220 Second, 408 Third. Scrapped at Rosyth from 1935.

***Laurentic*** (1927–1940). Harland & Wolff, Belfast. 11/1927. 18,724grt. 600 × 75.4ft. Twin triple expansion steam engines plus LP turbine. 15,000ihp (combined). 16 knots. Passengers 594 Cabin, 406 Tourist, 500 Third. Torpedoed and sunk by U99 off the Irish coast, 3 November 1940.

***Britannic*** (1930–1960). Harland & Wolff, Belfast. 5/1930. 26,943grt. 712 × 82.3ft. Twin 10 cylinder 4SC DA H&W – B&W oil engines. 17,000bhp. 18.5 knots. Passengers 504 Cabin, 551 Tourist, 498 Third. Scrapped at Inverkeithing from 1961.

***Georgic*** (1932–1941, 1950–1955). Ministry of War Transport (1941–1950). Harland & Wolff, Belfast. 6/1932. 27,759grt. 711 × 82.3ft. Twin 10 cylinder 4SC DA H.&W. – B.&W. oil engines. 17,000bhp. 18.5 knots. Passengers 479 Cabin, 557 Tourist, 506 Third. Scrapped at Faslane from 1956.

# Cunard White Star Line

**Queen Mary** (1936–1967). John Brown & Co. Ltd, Glasgow. 4/1936. 81,235grt. 1,019 × 118.1ft. Sixteen steam turbines SR geared to 4 shafts. 212,000shp. 28.5 knots. Passengers 776 Cabin, 784 Tourist, 579 Third. Sold to city of Long Beach, California, August 1967. At present preserved as a major tourist attraction, comprising shipping museum, hotel and convention centre.

***Mauretania*** (1939–1965). Cammell Laird & Co. Ltd, Birkenhead. 5/1939. 35,738grt. 772 × 89.6ft. Six steam turbines SR geared to 2 shafts. 42,000shp. 22 knots. Passengers 440 Cabin, 450 Tourist, 470 Third. Scrapped at Inverkeithing from 1965.

***Queen Elizabeth***, (1940–1972). John Brown & Co. Ltd, Glasgow. 2/1940. ***Seawise University*** (C Y Tung Group) 1970. 83,673grt. 1,031 × 118.4ft. Sixteen steam turbines SR geared to 4 shafts. 212,000shp – 28.5 knots; Passengers: 823 First, 662 Cabin, 798 Tourist. Destroyed by fire at Hong Kong on 9 January 1972 while undergoing conversion to floating university and cruise ship.

# APPENDIX II

## Annual North Atlantic Passenger Traffic Carryings, All Lines 1924–38 Inclusive

| | | | Westbound | | | | |
|---|---|---|---|---|---|---|---|
| Year | I | C | II | TC | III | Total | Trips |
| 1924 | 81,760 | 98,966 | 83,467 | ... | 193,944 | 458,137 | 969 |
| 1925 | 84,243 | 107,623 | 91,638 | ... | 228,872 | 512,376 | 1,006 |
| 1926 | 85,585 | 96,523 | 88,515 | 39,445 | 276,200 | 586,268 | 998 |
| 1927 | 88,654 | 92,245 | 74,747 | 73,296 | 301,239 | 630,181 | 1,026 |
| 1928 | 85,896 | 95,585 | 59,339 | 94,177 | 303,430 | 638,427 | 1,105 |
| 1929 | 87,043 | 91,294 | 53,152 | 111,634 | 303,011 | 646,134 | 1,078 |
| 1930 | 73,381 | 81,545 | 40,553 | 135,809 | 219,661 | 550,949 | 1,068 |
| 1931 | 54,770 | 47,337 | 19,521 | 97,694 | 88,817 | 308,139 | 889 |
| 1932 | 40,751 | 35,026 | 6,512 | 94,945 | 95,797 | 273,031 | 749 |
| 1933 | 31,920 | 31,219 | 3,525 | 75,288 | 83,062 | 225,014 | 708 |
| 1934 | 34,310 | 30,667 | 498 | 78,528 | 86,406 | 230,409 | 642 |
| 1935 | 36,366 | 32,375 | ... | 88,877 | 92,435 | 250,053 | 702 |
| 1936 | 2,432 | 80,038 | ... | 102,719 | 115,218 | 300,407 | 755 |
| 1937 | ... | 89,064 | ... | 114,668 | 139,751 | 343,483 | 782 |
| 1938 | ... | 72,167 | ... | 104,003 | 133,421 | 309,591 | 773 |
| Total | 787,111 | 1,081,674 | 521,467 | 1,211,083 | 2,661,264 | 6,262,599 | 13,250 |
| Average | 52,474 | 72,112 | 34,764 | 80,739 | 177,417 | 417,507 | 883 |

| | | | Eastbound | | | | |
|---|---|---|---|---|---|---|---|
| Year | I | C | II | TC | III | Total | Trips |
| 1924 | 71,806 | 77,674 | 54,697 | ... | 122,800 | 326,977 | 937 |
| 1925 | 75,710 | 77,441 | 49,081 | ... | 154,422 | 356,654 | 974 |
| 1926 | 74,666 | 70,485 | 46,507 | 41,097 | 127,243 | 359,998 | 946 |
| 1927 | 79,308 | 75,444 | 41,511 | 77,256 | 131,948 | 405,467 | 999 |
| 1928 | 76,425 | 79,315 | 35,806 | 90,870 | 139,904 | 422,320 | 1,079 |
| 1929 | 77,820 | 76,759 | 32,974 | 103,516 | 131,914 | 422,983 | 1,048 |
| 1930 | 64,017 | 74,259 | 29,925 | 123,627 | 159,576 | 451,404 | 1,057 |
| 1931 | 48,901 | 46,976 | 16,727 | 94,106 | 170,607 | 377,317 | 881 |
| 1932 | 37,666 | 35,530 | 5,971 | 99,137 | 191,374 | 369,678 | 747 |
| 1933 | 27,119 | 28,909 | 3,243 | 69,746 | 113,589 | 242,606 | 703 |
| 1934 | 30,255 | 28,424 | 379 | 71,150 | 99,511 | 229,719 | 638 |
| 1935 | 32,605 | 31,718 | ... | 82,124 | 101,568 | 248,015 | 700 |
| 1936 | 2,658 | 76,274 | ... | 92,947 | 125,363 | 297,242 | 747 |
| 1937 | ... | 83,210 | ... | 99,727 | 132,351 | 315,288 | 764 |
| 1938 | ... | 59,970 | ... | 79,495 | 118,887 | 258,352 | 784 |
| Total | 698,956 | 922,388 | 316,821 | 74,987 | 2,021,057 | 5,084,020 | 13,004 |
| Average | 46,597 | 61,493 | 21,121 | 1,124,798 | 134,737 | 338,935 | 867 |

I – First Class
C – Cabin Class
II – Second Class
TC – Tourist Third Class
III – Third Class

## Westbound and Eastbound Combined

| Year | I | C | II | TC | III | Total | Trips |
|---|---|---|---|---|---|---|---|
| 1924 | 153,566 | 176,640 | 138,164 | . . . | 316,744 | 785,114 | 1,906 |
| 1925 | 159,953 | 185,064 | 140,719 | . . . | 383,294 | 869,030 | 1,980 |
| 1926 | 160,251 | 167,008 | 135,022 | 80,542 | 403,443 | 946,266 | 1,944 |
| 1927 | 167,962 | 167,689 | 116,258 | 150,552 | 433,187 | 1,035,648 | 2,025 |
| 1928 | 162,321 | 174,900 | 95,145 | 185,047 | 443,334 | 1,060,747 | 2,184 |
| 1929 | 164,863 | 168,053 | 86,126 | 215,150 | 434,925 | 1,069,117 | 2,126 |
| 1930 | 137,398 | 155,804 | 70,478 | 259,436 | 379,237 | 1,002,353 | 2,125 |
| 1931 | 103,671 | 94,313 | 36,248 | 191,800 | 259,424 | 685,456 | 1,770 |
| 1932 | 78,417 | 70,556 | 12,483 | 194,082 | 287,171 | 642,709 | 1,496 |
| 1933 | 59,039 | 60,128 | 6,768 | 145,034 | 196,651 | 467,620 | 1,411 |
| 1934 | 64,565 | 59,091 | 877 | 149,678 | 185,917 | 460,128 | 1,280 |
| 1935 | 68,971 | 64,093 | . . . | 171,001 | 194,003 | 498,068 | 1,402 |
| 1936 | 5,090 | 156,312 | . . . | 195,666 | 240,581 | 597,649 | 1,502 |
| 1937 | . . . | 172,274 | . . . | 214,395 | 272,102 | 658,771 | 1,546 |
| 1938 | . . . | 132,137 | . . . | 183,498 | 252,308 | 567,943 | 1,557 |
| Total | 1,486,067 | 2,004,062 | 838,288 | 2,335,881 | 4,682,321 | 11,346,619 | 26,254 |
| Average | 99,071 | 133,604 | 55,886 | 155,725 | 312,155 | 756,441 | 1,750 |

# APPENDIX III

# White Star & Cunard Liners and the Blue Riband of the North Atlantic

Some record North Atlantic passages both East- and Westbound from 1923 onwards.
* = Record Blue Riband passage.
H = Holders of the Hales Trophy (1935 onwards).

| Date | | Ship | From | To | Distance nautical miles | Days hours minutes | Average speed knots |
|------|------|------|------|-----|-----|-----|-----|
| September | 1923 | Majestic | Ambrose | Cherbourg | 3104 | 5. 5.21 | 24.76 |
| August | 1924 | Mauretania | Ambrose | Cherbourg | 3198 | 5. 1.49 | 26.25* |
| August | 1928 | Mauretania | Cherbourg | Ambrose | 3164 | 5. 3.17 | 25.63 |
| August | 1928 | Mauretania | Ambrose | Eddystone | 3091 | 4.21.44 | 26.20 |
| July | 1929 | Bremen | Cherbourg | Ambrose | 3164 | 4.17.42 | 27.83* |
| July | 1929 | Bremen | Ambrose | Plymouth | 3084 | 4.14.30 | 27.91* |
| August | 1929 | Mauretania | Cherbourg | Ambrose | 3147 | 4.21.44 | 26.90 |
| August | 1929 | Mauretania | Ambrose | Plymouth | 3098 | 4.17.50 | 27.22 |
| March | 1930 | Europa | Cherbourg | Ambrose | 3157 | 4.17. 6 | 27.91* |
| October | 1932 | Rex | Ambrose | Gibraltar | 3163 | 5. 3.19 | 25.65 |
| May | 1933 | Conte di Savoia | Gibraltar | Ambrose | 3170 | 4.19.10 | 27.53 |
| May | 1933 | Bremen | Ambrose | Cherbourg | 3200 | 4.17.43 | 28.14* |
| June | 1933 | Bremen | Ambrose | Cherbourg | 3199 | 4.16.15 | 28.51* |
| August | 1933 | Rex | Gibraltar | Ambrose | 3188 | 4.13.58 | 28.92* H |
| August | 1934 | Empress of Britain | Fatherpoint (St Lawrence) | Cherbourg | | 4. 6.58 | 25.08 |
| May | 1935 | Normandie | Cowes | Ambrose | 3192 | 4.11.42 | 29.64* H |
| | | | Bishops Rock | Ambrose | 2971 | 4. 3.14 | 29.94* H |
| June | 1935 | Normandie | Ambrose | Bishops Rock | 3015 | 4. 3.28 | 30.31* H |
| May | 1936 | Queen Mary | Cherbourg | Ambrose | 3158 | 4.12.24 | 29.13 |
| July | 1936 | Queen Mary | Cherbourg | Ambrose | 3098 | 4. 8.37 | 29.61 |
| July | 1936 | Queen Mary | Ambrose | Cherbourg | 3128 | 4. 9. 0 | 29.79 |
| August | 1936 | Queen Mary | Cherbourg | Ambrose | 3097 | 4. 7.12 | 30.01 |
| | | | Bishops Rock | Ambrose | 2907 | 4. 0.27 | 30.14 |
| August | 1936 | Queen Mary | Ambrose | Cherbourg | 3129 | 4. 6.20 | 30.57* |
| | | | Ambrose | Bishops Rock | 2939 | 3.23.57 | 30.63* |
| March | 1937 | Normandie | Ambrose | Bishops Rock | 2978 | 4. 0. 6 | 30.99* H |
| April | 1937 | Aquitania | Ambrose | Cherbourg | 3198 | 5. 8.37 | 24.87 |
| August | 1938 | Normandie | Bishops Rock | Ambrose | 2906 | 3.23.36 | 30.58* H |
| August | 1938 | Normandie | Ambrose | Bishops Rock | 2926 | 3.22. 7 | 31.20* H |
| August | 1938 | Queen Mary | Bishops Rock | Ambrose | 2907 | 3.21.48 | 30.99* |
| August | 1938 | Queen Mary | Ambrose | Bishops Rock | 2938 | 3.20.42 | 31.69* |

# Chronology of Contemporary Events

| | | |
|---|---|---|
| 1929 | General | BBC commences experimental television programmes |
| | February | St Valentine's Day massacre – Al Capone at the height of his power |
| | July | Bremen *captures the Atlantic Blue Riband, westbound at a speed of 27.83 knots, eastbound at a* speed of 27.92 knots |
| | August | Airship *Graf Zeppelin* circumnavigates the world |
| | October | Wall Street stock market crash |
| 1930 | March | Europa *captures Atlantic Blue Riband, westbound at a speed of 27.91 knots* |
| | October | Airship R101 crashes on maiden flight |
| | December | *Keel of Cunard liner No 534 laid at Clydebank* |
| 1931 | General | Financial crisis growing and mounting unemployment in Europe as a result of the world depression |
| | January | *Keel of French liner* Normandie *laid at St Nazaire* |
| | August | *Italian liner* Rex *launched* |
| | September | Britain wins the Schneider Trophy outright; Japan invades Manchuria |
| 1932 | August | Jim Mollison flies the Atlantic in 30 hours |
| | September | *Maiden voyage of Italian liner* Rex |
| | October | *French liner* Normandie *launched* |
| | November | Franklin Delano Roosevelt elected President of USA |
| 1933 | January | Adolf Hitler appointed Chancellor of Germany |
| | July | Wiley Post flies solo around the world in 7 days and 18 hours |
| | August | Rex *captures Atlantic Blue Riband, westbound at a speed of 28.92 knots* |
| | December | Repeal of US Prohibition Laws |
| 1934 | August | On death of Hindenburg, Hitler becomes the President of Germany |
| | September | KLM establishes the longest air route to date – 9000 miles from Amsterdam to Batavia (Djakarta) |
| | | *Cunard liner* Queen Mary *launched* |
| 1935 | General | Watson-Watt invents Radar |
| | April | *Cunard liner* Mauretania *sold for scrap* |
| | May | Normandie *captures Atlantic Blue Riband, westbound at a speed of 29.98 knots, eastbound at a speed of 30.31 knots* |
| | September | *White Star liner* Olympic *sold for scrap* |
| | October | Italy invades Ethiopia |
| 1936 | General | First Butlin's holiday camp opened at Skegness; BBC start regular television programmes |
| | January | Death of King George V; accession of King Edward VIII |
| | February | *White Star liner* Homeric *sold for scrap* |
| | May | *White Star liner* Majestic *sold for scrap – resold for conversion to boys' training ship based at Rosyth; maiden voyage of the Cunard liner* Queen Mary |
| | July | Outbreak of Spanish Civil War |
| | August | Queen Mary *captures the Atlantic Blue Riband, westbound at a speed of 30.14 knots, eastbound at a* speed of 30.63 knots |
| | October | Jarrow hunger march |
| | December | Abdication of King Edward VIII; accession of King George VI; *keel of Cunard liner* Queen Elizabeth *laid at Clydebank* |

| | | |
|---|---|---|
| 1937 | General | First jet-engine operational |
| | March | Imperial Airways' Empire flying boat service inaugurated from Southampton with Shorts 'C' class aeroplanes |
| | May | Airship *Hindenburg* crashes at Lakehurst, New Jersey |
| | July | Japan resumes attacks on China |
| | July/August | Normandie *regains the Atlantic Blue Riband, westbound at a speed of 30.58 knots, eastbound at a speed of 31.20 knots* |
| 1938 | General | Introduction of nylon, ball-point pens and fluorescent lighting |
| | March | Germany annexes Austria |
| | May | Crisis over German occupation of Sudetenland |
| | August | Queen Mary *regains the Atlantic Blue Riband, westbound at a speed of 30.99 knots, eastbound at a speed of 31.69 knots* |
| | September | Munich agreement over Czechoslovakia heralded as 'Peace in our Time'; *Cunard liner* Queen Elizabeth *launched* |
| | November | *Cunard liner* Berengaria *sold for scrap* |
| 1939 | General | First jet-engined aircraft in Germany; first helicopter in USA |
| | March | End of Spanish Civil War |
| | September | Germany invades Poland – outbreak of World War II |

# SELECT BIBLIOGRAPHY

ANDERSON, ROY  White Star (T Stephenson & Sons Ltd 1964)

BONSOR, N R P  North Atlantic Seaway – 2nd edn, Vols I and II (David & Charles 1976)

CARY, ALAN L  Giant Liners (Sampson Low, Marston & Co. Ltd ca 1938)

CARY, ALAN L  Famous Liners and Their Stories (Sampson Low, Marston & Co. Ltd ca 1938)

CORSON, F REID  The Atlantic Ferry in the Twentieth Century (Sampson Low, Marston & Co. Ltd 1930)

EMMONS, FREDERICK  The Atlantic Liners 1925–1970 (David & Charles 1972)

LE FLEMING, H M  Cunard White Star Liners of the 1930s (Ian Allan, 1960)

HARDY, A C  British Ships Illustrated (A & C Black Ltd 1933)

HUGHES, TOM  The Blue Riband of the Atlantic (Patrick Stephens Ltd 1973)

HUNTER, K P and ROGERS, R J, LIEUTENANTS  H.M.S. *Caledonia*, The Royal Naval Engineering School – A Short History (1984)

KERR, ROSE  The Cruise of the *Calgaric* (Girl Guide Association 1933)

KLUDAS, ARNOLD  Great Passenger Ships of the World, Vols I–IV (Patrick Stephens Ltd 1975–77)

MALLETT, ALAN S and BELL, ANDREW M  The Pirrie – Kylsant Motorships 1915–1932 (Mallett & Bell Publishers 1984)

MITCHELL, W H *et al.*  A History of the White Star Line at Southampton (World Ship Society, Southampton Branch 1980)

OLDHAM, WILTON J  The Ismay Line (Charles Birchall & Sons 1961)

POTTER, NEIL and FROST, JACK  The *Queen Mary* (George G. Harrap 1971)

TALBOT-BOOTH, E C  His Majesty's Merchant Navy (Sampson Low, Marston & Co. Ltd ca 1942)

TODD, JOHN A  The Shipping World (Sir Isaac Pitman & Sons Ltd 1929)

WHITE, A G HORTON  Ships of the North Atlantic (Sampson Low, Marston & Co. Ltd ca 1939)

WILLIAMS, DAVID L and DE KERBRECH, RICHARD P  Damned by Destiny (Teredo Books Ltd 1982)

WILLIAMS, DAVID L, and DE KERBRECH RICHARD P  Atlantic Greyhounds (Series in *Ships Monthly*, July 1974–November 1975)

WILSON, V S FELLOWES  The Largest Ships of the World (Crosby Lockwood & Son 1926)

WILSON, R M  The Big Ships (Cassell & Co. 1956)

The Cunard Line – A Post War History (Blackjack Supplement – World Ship Society, Southampton Branch 1973)

# INDEX